Attention to Detail is Everything!
~ Drew Chitiea

This 6th Edition 2025, incorporates recent (January 2025) changes in FAA guidance for CFI expiration & renewal, Knowledge Test endorsements, and endorsement changes reflected in AC 61.65J.

All CFI's are encouraged to join the
The Society of Aviation and Flight Educators (SAFE)
www.SAFEpilots.org

I0081565

All CFI's are also encouraged to become Master Instructors.
www.MasterInstructors.org

Contacting the author about this book and other products, mountain flying and instruction in Colorado and general aviation consulting may be accessed via the author's website at:

www.ColoradoSkymaster.com

Drew Chitiea
PO Box 246
Watkins, CO 80137-0246

If found, please return to:

CFI Name_____

CFI Telephone Number_____

Retain until (date)_____ / _____ / _____

The Flight Instructor's Guide to Endorsements, IACRA & the TSA

With Sections for
CFI & CFI-SP Record-Keeping,
TSA Training & Certification
and BFR/IPC Records

Drew Chitiea
FAA Designated Pilot Examiner (retired)
Master CFI - Emeritus

6th Edition 2025

The Flight Instructor's Guide to Endorsements, IACRA & the TSA
6th Edition 2025

ISBN: 979-8-218-60669-5

TABLE OF CONTENTS

NEW FAA RULE REGARDING CFI RENEWAL

As of the time of this 6th edition, (1 December 2024), the FAA published a final rule eliminating expiration dates on Flight Instructor certificates. This will "increase efficiency, cut costs, and put instructor certificates in line with other airman certificates" which have no expiration date.

Under the new ruling, instructors must still renew certificate privileges every 24 calendar months by completing – and documenting – a Flight Instructor Refresher Course (FIRC), obtaining another instructor certificate, or engaging in further instructional activities. These must include at least 15 flight activities recognized by FAA-sponsored pilot proficiency programs. At the time of publication, it is unknown what these activities are, who can administer them, or how they will be documented to FAA's satisfaction.

The pre-existing requirements to obtain a 'Gold Seal' flight instructor certificate – recommending at least five applicants for a practical exam with the passage rate of 80% or better within the preceding 24 calendar months – will qualify for the renewal of flight instructor privileges.

It is recommended every flight instructor refer to trustworthy information sources to determine exact requirements for experience documentation and the reporting of same to the FAA when approaching the 24-calendar month privilege renewal time requirement.

For a flight instructor certificate without an expiration date:
[date] /s/ J. J. Jones 987654321CFI REED 12-31-2026

For a flight instructor certificate with an expiration date: [date] /s/ J. J. Jones 987654321CFI Exp. 01-31-2025
For a ground instructor: [date] /s/ J. J. Jones 987654321

NEW FAA PROCEDURE FOR FAA FOI KNOWLEDGE TESTS

Correcting an oversight concerning a Flight Instructor candidate taking the Fundamentals of Instruction (FOI) knowledge test without holding a recommendation (endorsement) from an authorized instructor, the FAA now requires "... a logbook endorsement or written statement from an authorized ground or flight instructor" be in possession of the applicant, and presented to the test center personnel, prior to taking the FOI knowledge test.

This rule became effective 1 September 2024. This endorsement has long been published within this volume on page 76 – Flight Instructor Aeronautical Knowledge Test 1.

FORWARD

The Flight Instructor check ride is arguably the most exacting and demanding in General Aviation. The ground portion is lengthy and challenging. Knowledge base is extensively tested, teaching ability is evaluated, understanding of protocols and procedures is examined, and comprehension of rules and regulations is viewed critically. Among the last, but not the least, of the applicant's concerns is paperwork.

As a Retired FAA Designated Pilot Examiner (DPE) I have seen many 'creative' endorsements made by Flight Instructors; often I wondered just what the student had received an endorsement for! The FAR's dictate precise endorsements by Flight Instructors and for exactly that reason are they are subject to testing. Although paperwork is regarded as the bane of every Flight Instructors' existence, it must be accomplished properly!

This book was created to assist Flight Instructors in managing the endorsement responsibilities placed on us by the FAA. All endorsements are in order of use for the respective certificates and/or ratings. Notes accompany most of them to assist and guide the instructor.

The CFI Records pages section accomplishes the requirements of the CFI Records Rule AND has proven acceptable to the FAA when applying for The Gold Seal Instructor designation or CFI renewal based on activity.

The BFR/IPC section serves as a 'reminder file' when client required refreshers are due.

The TSA CFI Training Section provides a place to record the initial and recurrent TSA security training required of all CFI's.

The TSA Citizen Student Endorsement Section provides a location to record the U.S. citizenship verification endorsement required prior to beginning flight training. This single volume will prove its worth in many areas of paperwork concern, all of which is required of us by the FAA.

REMEMBER:

When the weight of the paperwork equals the weight of the airplane,
YOU are almost ready to fly!

ACKNOWLEDGEMENTS

'Way back in the last century (and last millennium as well) when I was a green instructor, the Chief Pilot was Marv Hamlin (who was an instructor when God was a cadet) and the check-pilot was Ray Eastes, Lt. Col. USAF, both now 'Gone West.' I learned so much about flying, teaching and aviation from them because they were "Old School" pilots. They reinforced the "Do it right the first time" attitude instilled in me by my parents, who I also acknowledge for their support and encouragement.

This book, I trust, will pass on the guidance and standards those men gave to me so that other instructors can bring to the next generation of pilots a respect and willingness to do things correctly. As Coach DeBerry, now retired from the USAF Academy, once said: "You do the right thing: Every Play, Every Day." THAT is a formula for success.

I also thank all the CFI's who contributed to the prior editions of this book making it a success and the standard for proper and precise endorsements. Many of their comments and suggestions are contained in this, the sixth edition, and for that I thank you all.

And to my dear wife Peggy Ann Long [1946 - 2015] whose computer skills, publishing connections and encouragement - occasionally accompanied by a swift kick to my tailfeathers - got this book out the door 'way back when.

Drew Chitiea – Master CFI Emeritus
FAA DPE (ret.)
Centennial, Colorado
January 2025

ABOUT THE AUTHOR

Drew Chitiea was introduced to aviation at age eight when he and his family were airlifted out of a New Zealand meadow. Living and working in the sky since 1969, he holds an ATP certificate with all fixed-wing Flight and Ground Instructor ratings.

His forte is Tailwheel and Aerobatics training with extensive time as a Mountain Pilot & Instructor in the Colorado Rockies. Insurance- required training and Technologically Advanced Airplanes (TAA's) are also a specialty. He is credited with 130 Search-and-Rescue (SAR) missions, flown as a bush pilot in Alaska, performed as a low-level air show pilot, instructed at a major airline, was chief pilot for a Part 141 airline training college and a Check Pilot at the USAF Academy. Currently he is an experimental airplane flight test pilot and corporate pilot. He has extensive experience in vintage and experimental airplanes and to date has logged flight time in over 200 different make & models of airplanes.

He is a FAA Gold Seal instructor, FAA FASTeam member, published aviation author, and was awarded the honorific "Master Aviation Instructor – Emeritus" after holding a flight instructor certificate for over 45 years. He is a retired Designated Pilot Examiner (DPE) in Colorado specializing in training pilots to gain their Flight Instructor certificate.

Visit his website at
www.ColoradoSkymaster.com

HOW TO BEST UTILIZE THIS BOOK

1. KEEP this book in your flight bag. REFER to this book EVERY time you make an endorsement. Do NOT rely on memory alone for the correct wording. The "TLAR Method" ("That Looks About Right") doesn't cut it. Many logbooks have pre-printed endorsements in the back but, depending on the age of the logbook, the FARs mentioned may be out-of-date and thus incorrect.

2. IMMEDIATELY after you have made the endorsement, record it in the CFI Records section of this book. Remember, a record of particular endorsements is REQUIRED by the FAA to be kept by the instructor.

3. The Flight Review/Instrument Proficiency Check section of this book is to record those events. THEN, occasionally review the dates, call your students/clients and remind them the next one is due.

4. IMMEDIATELY following your TSA initial and/or recurrent training, record that fact in the TSA section of this book. It will serve not only as evidence of your participation but will provide a reminder of when the next training is due.

5. Refer to the TSA Guidance section BEFORE beginning the flight training of anyone. YOU are by legal definition a 'flight school' and have certain responsibilities per Transportation Security Regulations (TSR's). And, they have zero sense of humor if their regulations are not followed to the letter.

6. FAA certification branch now strongly recommends using

the Integrated Airman Certification and Rating Application (IACRA) method when applying for a certificate and/or rating. While the old paper FAA forms 8710-1 & 8710-11 may still be used, the preferred method is now applying via IACRA. Refer to the section covering the use of IACRA for guidance to both Recommending Instructors (RI) and applicants. Once you get the hang of it, you may very well prefer this method. Of course, you'll need a computer with internet access via either Internet Explorer or Mozilla Firefox (at this time, the only two Internet Service Provider's supported at the FAA).

7. **KEEP THIS BOOK!** The CFI Records must be kept for three (3) years but TSA records kept for five (5) years! Go figure! Again, required of all CFI's by regulation.

8. Take this book to your local FSDO when you meet the requirements of the Gold Seal designation (8 out of 10 applicants passing their flightcheck the first time) or wish to renew your CFI based on activity. Your carefully kept records will ease and speed along the process!

CFI TSA TRAINING VALIDATION RULE

TSA Help Desk
(571) 227-1004
AFSP.Help@dhs.gov
Monday - Friday
0800 - 1700 Eastern time

ALL flight, ground and simulator instructors and those persons likely to come into contact with flight students [counter persons and administrative personnel included] are required to undergo initial and recurrent security awareness training approved by the TSA prior to coming into contact with those flight students. If you, as a CFI, are working through a flight school, that school will require proof of training as detailed below for you to legally work there. If you are an independent CFI, you are legally defined as a 'flight school' and so must comply with the training and record-keeping requirements detailed below. That's a post 9/11 fact of life, folks.

Accomplish the on-line training course; when completed you will be able to print a Certificate of Training. Provide a copy of that to your flight school [make a note in the TSA CFI section of this book] and retain the certificate as proof that the initial course of security awareness training has been accomplished.

Initial and recurrency training courses can be found at the AOPA, King Schools, TSA, and other aviation services websites.

Within this website are several links for security awareness retraining and, after completing the course, a certificate so stating completion of the annual retraining course. Provide a copy of the recurrent training to your flight school annually in the anniversary month you took your initial TSA training [or as required by the flight school]. If you are an independent CFI, keep a copy of the certificate of training in your records and/or record that fact in the TSA CFI portion of this book.

U.S. CITIZEN FLIGHT TRAINING PROTOCOLS

BEFORE a United States citizen can begin flight training towards an *initial* FAA pilot certificate [Recreational, Sport or Private; an Instrument rating or Multi-engine rating] the flight school must verify citizenship.

1. **Applicability:** Determining citizenship status pertains *only* to flight training for an *initial* FAA pilot certificate [Sport, Recreational or Private] and to the Instrument and/or Multi-engine ratings.

2. **Proof of Citizenship:** The prospective student must produce evidence of United States citizenship with one of the following:
   a) Valid, unexpired United States passport
   b) Original and government-issued birth certificate of the United States, American Samoa or the Swains Islands
   c) Original certificate of United States citizenship with raised seal [Form N-560 or N-561]
   d) Original United States Naturalization Certificate with raised seal [Form N-550 or N-570]
   e) All the above (a - d) also include presenting government issued photo identification

US Citizen Record-Keeping Requirement *Logbook and/or Record-Keeping Requirements.* A flight school *must* do ONE of the following:

1. Keep copies of the documents used to provide proof of citizenship for five (5) years.

2. Make an endorsement in the instructor's logbook or other record used by the instructor to record flight student endorsements [see TSA CITIZEN STUDENT ENDORSEMENT section of this book] attesting to the fact they [the CFI] have inspected the citizenship documents provided by the student pilot.

3. Make the following endorsement in the Student Pilot's logbook:

> "I certify that [insert student's name] has presented me with a [insert type of document presented], control number [insert relevant control or identification number] establishing the he/she is a United States citizen [or national] in accordance with 49 CFR 1552.3(h)." Date, CFI Signature, CFI number, and expiration date.

The above proof-of-citizenship requirements do NOT apply to Flight Reviews [BFR], Instrument Proficiency checks [IPC], introductory flights, tailwheel training, high performance and/or complex aircraft training or any other ground and/or flight check to review rules, manoeuvres, procedures, or to demonstrate existing pilot skills utilizing aircraft with MTOW of 12,500 pounds or less.

NON-U.S. CITIZEN FLIGHT TRAINING PROTOCOLS

Non-US citizens desiring flight training in the United States must be vetted by the TSA prior to initiating any flight training. To do so, the following steps must be achieved before commencing any flight training:

BOTH the flight training provider AND the flight training applicant must have a valid and active email address to respond to TSA information and messages.

(NOTE: This could be a frustrating process, so be sure to review the FAQ's first to obtain better overview of how the system works prior to throwing the computer out the window.)

1. Flight training provider must be registered with the TSA [includes independent CFI's]
   www.flightschoolcandidates.gov

2. Student creates a "New Student Account" at:
   https://www.flightschoolcandidates.gov/afsp2/?acct_type=p &section =WN [top right of page] and submits a training request to the TSA

3. Flight training provider confirms the student's request.

4. Student remits a non-refundable processing fee to the TSA.

5. Flight training provider and the student receive preliminary TSA decision, usually within 30 days.

6. Student submits fingerprints via approved format to TSA. There are requirements for the fingerprinting process found at: www.flightschoolcandidates.gov

7. TSA confirms receipt of fingerprint data and processing fee; provisional approval to commence flight training.

8. Student photo taken on first day of training sent to TSA.

9. TSA notifies flight training provider if training must cease.

10. Okay to commence/continue flight training.

Non-Citizen Record-Keeping Required of Flight Schools and/or Independent Instructors:

1. Student training record

2. Student photo taken at commencement of flight training

3. TSA approval notification

4. Name, gender and date of birth of the student

5. TSA ID number

6. Copy of student passport [current and previous] and visas

7. Student's country of birth and citizenship, including any previous countries of citizenship

8. Requested type(s), location(s) and date(s) of training

9. Copy of U.S. pilot certificate(s) and number(s), if any

10. Student address(es) and phone number(s) over past 5 years

11. Copy of TSA processing fee payment receipt.

12.

THE CFI's GUIDE TO THE INTEGRATED AIRMAN CERTIFICATION & RATING APPLICATION (IACRA)

1. Overview

IACRA is a web-based application that minimizes the necessity of paper airman certification/rating application forms such as the 8710-1 and 8710-11. IACRA electronically records and validates information required to complete the airman application and the other certification documents including the appropriate temporary airman certificate and knowledge test results. It corroborates information from multiple FAA databases and automatically ensures that applicants meet regulatory and policy requirements. It uses digital signatures throughout the certification process which brings the application in compliance with the Government Paperwork Elimination Act.

2. Roles

IACRA uses 'roles' to determine levels of access granted to the user by validating an individual's FAA credentials electronically. Each time an IACRA user, other than an applicant, chooses a role and completes the registration the information is verified against the various FAA databases in order to determine authorization.

There are several roles for FAA-approved (Part 141/142) training centers, however the most prevalent roles used in part 61 flight schools using IACRA are defined below:

Role	*Description*
• Applicant	Any person applying for an airman certificate
• Recommending Instructor (RI)	Any person authorized to instruct applicants who considers the applicant ready for the practical test.
• Designated Pilot Examiner (DPE)	Any person authorized to conduct practical tests and issue airman certificates
• Aviation Safety Inspector (ASI)	FAA personnel authorized to issue specific airman certificates

3. National Service Desk (NSD)

The National Service Desk is available when users have support issues with IACRA or other FAA supported programs. Users who have forgotten their password should attempt online or email password recovery prior to contacting the help desk (detailed later). If users are unable to recover their password using the IACRA password recovery options or are unable to find the information they need in the IACRA FAQs, they may contact the help desk at https://iacra.faa.gov/iacra/FAQ.aspx

> Hours of operations: 24 hours a day / 7 days a week
> Telephone number: Toll-Free 1- 844-322-6948
> E-mail address: 9-NATL-AVS-IT-ServiceDesk@FAA.GOV

4. Process Overview

It must be CLEARLY UNDERSTOOD that IACRA is supported by only two browser modes - Internet Explorer or Mozilla Firefox. Attempting to access IACRA through any other browser will not result in success.

a. Open IACRA with either browser: http://iacra.faa.gov/iacra
b. Chose 'Login' or 'Register' (if not already a registered user)
  • During registration, you will be asked to create a user name and a password. After fully registered, IACRA will issue to you a unique and permanent FAA Tracking Number (FTN).

•It is STRONGLY RECOMMENDED you place the FTN number, your user name and password in a place both secure AND where you can find it again - like in the back of your logbook.

c. When logging in, use the FTN, your user name and password to access your file at the FAA.

d. Follow the instructions for your role - each role has different information pathways.

e. CHECK and RE-CHECK all information entered PRIOR to electronically signing the application. Once signed by the applicant, no changes may be made to that application. A new application will be needed.

f. At the termination of the entire examination process, the application is digitally transmitted to the Airman Registry; the applicant is then issued a Temporary Certificate, a Notice of Disapproval or a Letter of Discontinuance, as appropriate.

5. Registration

a. When registering, all persons should select "Applicant" as in the future another certificate and/or rating may be applied for.

b. All flight instructors should select the 'Recommending Instructor" role; any other role may be selected as appropriate.

c. Certifying Officers and/or school administrators should select their role(s) as appropriate.

d. User Profile and Personal Information:
   • If you possess an airman certificate, enter the information requested.
   • Enter all personal information in the boxes shown. BE SURE to explore all drop-down menus for available information choices.
   • Permanent Mailing Address: If mail is delivered to a post office box, place the residential physical address in the 'physical description' box.
      e. Complete the remainder of the registration informational process.
      f. Create and enter your IACRA user name and password

(Again, place these two items in a secure and readily retrievable location - like the back of your logbook).
  g. IACRA will then acknowledge your successful registration by assigning you a unique FTN. Place that adjacent to your user name and password.

6. Creating an Application
a. Log-in to IACRA
b. Click on "Applicant"
c. Click on "Start New Application"
  • Under 1) Application Type:
    o Use the drop-down arrow to choose the appropriate type (pilot)
  • Under 2) Certifications:
    Again use drop-down arrow and choose the appropriate one. Most applicants will use the "Standard" selection and "Part 61" (completion of required test) unless in a Part 141 school, then choose that.

7. Confirm all Personal Information
It is important to record the exact physical address of residence; if mail is sent elsewhere, such as a PO Box, then note that under the "Special Mailing Address" section.

  • Continue to confirm or enter all personal information; use every drop-down menu to view the choices available.

8. Completion of Required Test - Aircraft to be used
I will tell you right now this will be the most frustrating part of the entire process. Most certificated aircraft can be found by using the search radio buttons of either make/model or name. But there will be some - especially Light Sport Aircraft (LSA) that cannot be found. Use the "SP-GEN" code or call the Help Desk at the phone number mentioned in the beginning of this section.
  • Even if applying for a Student Pilot certificate, Flight Instructor or ATP, it's a good idea to put in as accurate record of flight time as possible. If ever your logbook was lost or stolen, the

hours logged on the form will allow a rebuilding of your flight times as of the application date.

Important Information:

a. Your application cannot be submitted until all validation errors are corrected (all the upper tabs have green checkmarks in them).

b. Be SURE to review the application CAREFULLY and make any corrections PRIOR TO submitting it. If in doubt, your recommending instructor and/or evaluator can assist in checking for accuracy.

c. KNOW and/or have available your FTN number, user name and password; you will need to give the FTN number to both your recommending instructor and Examiner to proceed.

d. Questions to the National Service Desk can be submitted to:
9-NATL-AVS-IT-ServiceDesk@faa.gov or
1-844-322-6948

e. Record your application number where it can be retrieved if necessary.

f. Again, an application can be amended PRIOR TO submitting it; once submitted it can only be changed if the recommending instructor returns it to the applicant or an entirely new application must be completed.

ATTENTION TO DETAIL IS EVERYTHING!

9. Recommending Instructor Console

a. Log into IACRA as "Recommending Instructor"

b. Follow the Recommending Instructor's checklist
  • You will need the applicant's FTN number and, if entering the applicant's Knowledge Test data, the Knowledge Test code (long string of numbers) from the applicant's knowledge test report.

c. When signing the application as Recommending Instructor, on the blue "Click to Sign":

BENJAMIN LARRY AARON	Click to Sign	Cancel
	Here ↑	

10. Password Recovery

To avoid this process, it is **STRONGLY RECOMMENDED** that the applicant record their FTN number, user name and password in a safe and secure location, such as in the back of their logbook. It would behove the recommending instructor to insure their students, clients and applicants perform this to minimize frustration and/or anxiety when trying to locate that information.

- The password recovery function is located on the IACRA home page (www.iacra.faa.gov). The password can be recovered either on-line or via an email.
- If on-line recovery option is used, the user must supply the FTN number, user name or email address associated with the user account.
- The security questions answered when setting up the account must then be answered.
- The new password may then be entered. Be SURE to record the new password in a safe and secure location.
- The user may then return to the IACRA home page and log in using the new password.
- If the email option is used, a new temporary password will be emailed to the email address associated with the account.
- Upon log-in, the user will be asked to create a new password. Be SURE to record the new password in a safe and secure location.

11. Keeping a User's Account Up-to-date

It is imperative the user's personal information be kept up-to-date. To make changes in the user's account (User Profile, Add/Remove/Change roles, Edit preferences, change Password, etc.):

- First log into IACRA and then select the area of information change(s) required.

PRESOLO AERONAUTICAL KNOWLEDGE
FAR 61.35 (a) & 61.87 (b)

"Mr./Ms._____, certificate # _____, has completed a presolo written exam required by 61.87 (b) demonstrating knowledge of PAR's 61 and 91 applicable to student pilots, airspace rules and procedures at (airport), flight characteristics and operational limitations of a (aircraft make and model)."

For a flight instructor certificate **without** an expiration date:
[date] /s/ J. J. Jones 987654321CFI REED 12-31-2026

For a flight instructor certificate **with** an expiration date:
[date] /s/ J. J. Jones 987654321CFI Exp. 01-31-2025

CFI NOTES:

The student's authorized instructor must administer the exam and review all incorrect answers before authorizing solo flight.

The CFI is required to keep a record of the results of this test. Ed. - It's a Knowledge Test.

(Use the CFI Records section of this book.)

PRESOLO FLIGHT TRAINING (1st Solo)
FAR 61.87 (n)

"I certify that I have given Mr./Ms. _____, certificate # _____, the flight instruction required by FAR 61.87 (c) in a (aircraft make and model). He/she has demonstrated satisfactory proficiency and safety in the applicable manoeuvres listed in FAR 61.87* and is competent to make solo flights in a (aircraft make and model) subject to the following limitations: (Wind direction and velocity, crosswind component, weather and any other limitations) Solo privileges expire on (Date)."

For a flight instructor certificate **without** an expiration date:
[date] /s/ J. J. Jones 987654321CFI REED 12-31-2026

For a flight instructor certificate **with** an expiration date:
[date] /s/ J. J. Jones 987654321CFI Exp. 01-31-2025

CFI NOTES:

The authorized instructor who provided the training must make this endorsement & must abide by the limitations in FAR 61.87(p).

Ensure the medical certificate is endorsed for aircraft make and model!

Assure that solo privileges expiration date is 90 days from the endorsement date, not to same date three calendar months later.
* Maneuvers prescribed in FAR 61.87 for:

(d) Single-engine airplane	*(i) Glider*
(e) Multi-engine airplane	*(j) Balloon*
(f) Helicopter	*(k) Airship*
(g) Gyroplane	*(l) Powered parachute*
(h) Powered-lift	*(m) Weight-shift control aircraft*

90 DAY SOLO ENDORSEMENT (Other than 1st Solo)

FAR 61.87 (n)

"I certify that I have given Mr./Ms. _____, certificate # _____, the flight instruction required by FAR 61.87 (n). He/she meets the requirements of FAR 61.87 * and is competent to make safe solo flights in a (aircraft make and model) subject to the following limitations: (Wind direction and velocity, crosswind component, weather and any other limitations). Solo privileges expire on (Date)."

For a flight instructor certificate **without** an expiration date:
[date] /s/ J. J. Jones 987654321CFI REED 12-31-2026

For a flight instructor certificate **with** an expiration date:
[date] /s/ J. J. Jones 987654321CFI Exp. 01-31-2025

CFI NOTES:
This endorsement should be used for solo privileges past the first 90-day period of the Student Pilot 2 endorsement.

The authorized instructor who provided the training must make this endorsement & must abide by the limitations in FAR 61.87(p).

Ensure the medical certificate is endorsed for aircraft make and model!

Assure that solo privileges expiration date is 90 days from the endorsement date, not to same date three calendar months later.
* FAR 61.87 subsections are:

(d) Single-engine airplane	*(i) Glider*
(e) Multi-engine airplane	*(j) Balloon*
(f) Helicopter	*(k) Airship*
(g) Gyroplane	*(l) Powered parachute*
(h) Powered-lift	*(m) Weight-shift control aircraft*

STUDENT SOLO CROSS-COUNTRY
FAR 61.93 (c)(l)

"I certify I have given Mr./Ms._____, certificate # _____, the instruction required by FAR 61.93* and find his/her preflight planning and preparation is correct. He/she is proficient to make safe solo flight from (airport), landing at (airport) and (airport) and return in a (aircraft make and model) on (Date). Landings and takeoffs from (airport) or (airport) are subject to the following limitations: (Wind direction & velocity, crosswind component, weather & any other limitations)."

For a flight instructor certificate **without** an expiration date:
[date] /s/ J. J. Jones 987654321CFI REED 12-31-2026

For a flight instructor certificate **with** an expiration date:
[date] /s/ J. J. Jones 987654321CFI Exp. 01-31-2025

CFI NOTES:
The authorized instructor who provided the training must make this endorsement & must abide by the limitations in FAR 61.87(p) & FAR 61.93(d) as to permitting a Student Pilot solo cross-country flight.

Assure student's 90-day logbook endorsement is valid for aircraft make and model & the student's medical certificate is endorsed for cross-country flight with appropriate make and model. This endorsement must be entered into the Student Pitot's logbook for each and every solo cross-country the student intends to make.
* FAR 61.93 sub-sections are:

(
d) Single-engine airplane
(e) Multi-engine airplane
(f) Helicopter
(g) Gyroplane
(h) Powered-lift
(i) Glider

(j) Balloon
(k) Airship
(l) Powered parachute
(m) Weight-shift control aircraft

CFI REVIEW of STUDENT CROSS-COUNTRY PLANNING
FAR 61.93 (c)(2)(ii)

"I certify I have reviewed the cross-country planning of Mr./Ms. _____, certificate # _____, and find it correct for a flight under VFR conditions, that he/she is proficient to safely conduct the flight, landing at (airport) and (airport) and returning to (airport) on (Date) under the following limitations: (Wind direction & velocity, crosswind component, weather & any other limitations)."

For a flight instructor certificate **without** an expiration date:
[date] /s/ J. J. Jones 987654321CFI REED 12-31-2026

For a flight instructor certificate **with** an expiration date:
[date] /s/ J. J. Jones 987654321CFI Exp. 01-31-2025

CFI NOTES:

The instructor who provided the original cross-country training must make the Student Pilot 4 endorsement. This endorsement is for any CFI reviewing the cross-country planning of a Student Pilot.

The reviewing instructor must abide by the limitations listed in FAR 61.93(d) as to permitting a Student Pilot solo cross-country flight.

SOLO TAKEOFFS & LANDINGS AT ANOTHER AIRPORT WITHIN 25nm OF THE HOME-BASE AIRPORT
FAR61.93 (b)

"I certify I have given Mr./Ms._____, certificate # _____, instruction required by FAR 61.93(b)(l) and find him/her competent and proficient to practice takeoffs and landings at (airport) returning to (airport). Takeoffs and landings are subject to the following limitations: (Wind direction & velocity, crosswind component, & weather limitations)."

For a flight instructor certificate **without** an expiration date:
[date] /s/ J. J. Jones 987654321CFI REED 12-31-2026

For a flight instructor certificate **with** an expiration date:
[date] /s/ J. J. Jones 987654321CFI Exp. 01-31-2025

CFI NOTES:

Assure student's 90-day logbook endorsement is valid. Assure the Student's Medical certificate is endorsed for:

- *Solo flight*
- *Appropriate aircraft make/model and*
- *Cross-country flight*

The authorized instructor 1vho provided the training must make this endorsement & must abide by the limitations in FAR 61.87(p).

The reviewing instructor must abide by the limitations listed in FAR 61.93(d) as to permitting a Student Pilot solo cross-country flight

REPEATED STUDENT SOLO CROSS-COUNTRY FLIGHTS WITHIN 50 nm FROM THE HOME-BASE AIRPORT
FAR 61.93 (b)(2)

"I certify I have given Mr./Ms._____, certificate # _____, the flight instruction required by FAR 61.93(b)(2) from (airport) to (airport) and return. I find him/her proficient to conduct repeated solo cross-country flights in a (aircraft make and model) in both directions between those two airports, subject to the following limitations: (Wind direction & velocity, crosswind component, & weather limitations)."

For a flight instructor certificate **without** an expiration date:
[date] /s/ J. J. Jones 987654321CFI REED 12-31-2026

For a flight instructor certificate **with** an expiration date:
[date] /s/ J. J. Jones 987654321CFI Exp. 01-31-2025

CFI NOTES:

Assure that student's 90-day solo endorsement in logbook is valid. Assure the Student's Medical certificate is endorsed for:

- *Solo flight*
- *Appropriate aircraft make/model*
- *Cross-country flight*

This endorsement is not required for each student flight. The authorized instructor who provided the training must make this endorsement & must abide by the limitations in FAR 61.87(p).
The reviewing instructor must abide by the limitations listed in FAR 61.93(d) as to permitting a Student Pilot solo cross-country flight.

STUDENT CLASS B AIRSPACE 90-DAY
AIRSPACE OPERATIONS
FAR 61.89 (c)(4) & 61.95 (a)

"I certify that I have given Mr./Ms. _____, certificate # _____, ground and flight instruction required by FAR 61.95 (a) and find him/her proficient to conduct solo flight operations in (specific name) Class B airspace. Authority to operate in that airspace terminates on (Date)."

For a flight instructor certificate **without** an expiration date:
[date] /s/ J. J. Jones 987654321CFI REED 12-31-2026

For a flight instructor certificate **with** an expiration date:
[date] /s/ J. J. Jones 987654321CFI Exp. 01-31-2025

CFI NOTES:

Assure that Student's Medical Certificate is properly endorsed for solo and appropriate aircraft make and model.

Assure that the expiration date is 90 days from the endorsement date, not to same date three calendar months later!

The authorized instructor who provided the training must make this endorsement & must abide by the limitations in FAR 61.87(p).

FAR 91, Appendix D, Section 4 lists those airports at which Student Pilot activity is prohibited.

STUDENT CLASS B AIRSPACE 90-DAY
AIRPORT OPERATIONS
FAR 61.89 (c)(4)61.95 (b)

"I certify that I have given Mr./Ms. _____, certificate # _____, ground and flight instruction required by FAR 61.95(b) and find him/her proficient to conduct solo flight operations at (airport) in the (specific name) Class B airspace subject to the following limitations: (Wind direction & velocity, crosswind component, weather & any other limitations). Authority to operate at that airport expires on (Date)."

For a flight instructor certificate **without** an expiration date:
[date] /s/ J. J. Jones 987654321CFI REED 12-31-2026

For a flight instructor certificate **with** an expiration date:
[date] /s/ J. J. Jones 987654321CFI Exp. 01-31-2025

CFI NOTES:

Assure that Student's Medical Certificate is properly endorsed for solo and appropriate aircraft make and model.

Assure that the expiration date is 90 days from the endorsement date, not to same date three calendar months later!

FAR 91, Appendix D, Section 4 lists those airports at which Student Pilot activity is prohibited.

The authorized instructor who provided the training must make this endorsement & must abide by the limitations in FAR 61.87(p).

STUDENT PILOT - SEEKING SPORT or RECREATIONAL CERTIFICATE-OPERATIONS AT or WITHIN CLASS B/C/D AIRSPACE and/or AIRPORTS, or AIRPORTS WITH A CONTROL TOWER IN OTHER AIRSPACE.

FAR 61.94 (a)

"I certify that I have given Mr./Ms. _____, certificate # _____, ground and flight training required by FAR 61.94(a) in the applicable parts of part 91 pertaining to (specific name class B/C/D) airspace and (specific name class B/C/D) airport operations and find him/her proficient to conduct solo flight (in that airspace and/or that airport) under the following limitations: (Wind direction & velocity, crosswind component, & weather limitations) This authorization expires on (Date)."

For a flight instructor certificate **without** an expiration date:
[date] /s/ J. J. Jones 987654321CFI REED 12-31-2026

For a flight instructor certificate **with** an expiration date:
[date] /s/ J. J. Jones 987654321CFI Exp. 01-31-2025

CFI NOTES:

Assure the expiration date is 90 days from the issue date and not the same date three calendar months later.

The authorized instructor who provided the training must make this endorsement & must abide by the limitations in FAR 61.87(p).

STUDENT NIGHT SOLO
FAR 61.87 (o)

"I certify that I have given Mr./Ms. _____, certificate # _____, the flight training required by FAR 61.87 (o) and find him/her proficient to make safe night solo flights at (airport) in a (aircraft make and model) under the following conditions: (Wind direction & velocity, crosswind component, & weather limitations). This authorization expires on (Date)."

For a flight instructor certificate **without** an expiration date:
[date] /s/ J. J. Jones 987654321CFI REED 12-31-2026

For a flight instructor certificate **with** an expiration date:
[date] /s/ J. J. Jones 987654321CFI Exp. 01-31-2025

CFI NOTES:

Assure that Student's Medical Certificate is properly endorsed for aircraft make and model.

Assure the expiration date is 90 days from the issue date and not the same date three calendar months later.

The authorized instructor who provided the training must make this endorsement & must abide by the limitations in FAR 61.87(p).

RECREATIONAL PILOT

RECREATIONAL PILOT AERONAUTICAL KNOWLEDGE
FAR 61.35 (a)(l) & 61.96 (b)(3)

"I certify that I have given Mr./Ms._____, certificate # _____, ground instruction required by FAR 61.97 (b) and find him/her prepared to take the Recreational Pilot Knowledge test."

For a flight instructor certificate **without** an expiration date:
[date] /s/ J. J. Jones 987654321CFI REED 12-31-2026

For a flight instructor certificate **with** an expiration date:
[date] /s/ J. J. Jones 987654321CFI Exp. 01-31-2025

OR: If student has completed a home study course:

"I have reviewed the (specific name) home study course work of Mr./Ms._____, certificate # _____, and certify the requirements of FAR 61.97 (b) have been met and he/she is prepared for the Recreational Pilot Knowledge test."

For a flight instructor certificate **without** an expiration date:
[date] /s/ J. J. Jones 987654321CFI REED 12-31-2026

For a flight instructor certificate **with** an expiration date:
[date] /s/ J. J. Jones 987654321CFI Exp. 01-31-2025

CFI NOTES:

The authorized instructor who provided the training must make this endorsement.

RECREATIONAL PILOT FLIGHT PROFICIENCY
FAR 61.96 (b) 5

I certify that I have given Mr./Ms. _____, certificate # _____, the flight instruction required by FAR 61.98 (b)(*), and find him/her proficient to perform each pilot operation safely as a Recreational Pilot."

For a flight instructor certificate **without** an expiration date:
[date] /s/ J. J. Jones 987654321CFI REED 12-31-2026

For a flight instructor certificate **with** an expiration date:
[date] /s/ J. J. Jones 987654321CFI Exp. 01-31-2025

CFI NOTES:

The authorized instructor who provided the training must make this endorsement.

* FAR 61.98 (b) sub-sections are:
    (1) Single-engine airplane
    (2) Helicopter
    (3) Rotocraft gyroplane

PREREQUISITES FOR PRACTICAL TESTS
FAR 61.39 (a)(6)

"I certify that I have given Mr./Ms. _____, certificate # _____, the flight instruction required by FAR 61.39 (a)(6) within the preceding two calendar months and find him/her prepared for the exam. He/she has demonstrated satisfactory knowledge of the subject areas shown to be deficient on his/her Airman Knowledge Test."

For a flight instructor certificate **without** an expiration date:
[date] /s/ J. J. Jones 987654321CFI REED 12-31-2026

For a flight instructor certificate **with** an expiration date:
[date] /s/ J. J. Jones 987654321CFI Exp. 01-31-2025

CFI NOTES:
The authorized instructor who provided the training must make this endorsement.
Recreational Pilot endorsements 2 & 3 may be combined to read:

"I certify that I have given Mr./Ms. _____, certificate # _____, the flight instruction required by FAR 61.98 (b)(*) & FAR 61.39(a)(6) within the preceding two calendar months and find him/her proficient to perform each pilot operation safely as a Recreational Pilot. He/she has demonstrated satisfactory knowledge of the subject areas shown to be deficient on his/her Airman Knowledge Test."

*For a flight instructor certificate **without** an expiration date:*
[date] /s/ J. J. Jones 987654321CFI REED 12-31-2026

*For a flight instructor certificate **with** an expiration date:*
[date] /s/ J. J. Jones 987654321CFI Exp. 01-31-2025

* FAR 61.98(b) sub-sections are:
> *1. Single-engine airplane*
> *2. Helicopter*
> *3. Rotorcraft gyroplane*

RECREATIONAL PILOT *ACTING AS PIC* WITHIN 50nm OF AIRPORT WHERE INSTRUCTION WAS RECEIVED

FAR 61.101 (b)

"I certify I have given Mr./Ms. _____,certificate #_____, ground and the flight instruction required by FAR 61.101 (b) and find him/her proficient to operate a (<u>aircraft make and model</u>) for flight within a 50 nm radius of (<u>specific name</u>) airport."

For a flight instructor certificate **without** an expiration date:
[date] /s/ J. J. Jones 987654321CFI REED 12-31-2026

For a flight instructor certificate **with** an expiration date:
[date] /s/ J. J. Jones 987654321CFI Exp. 01-31-2025

CFI NOTES:

The authorized instructor who provided the training must make this endorsement.

This logbook endorsement MUST be in the pilots' possession or readily accessible in the aircraft when they fly.

RECREATIONAL PILOT ACTING AS PIC BEYOND 50 NM RADIUS FROM DEPARTURE AIRPORT
FAR 61.101 (c)

"I certify that I have given Mr./Ms. _____, certificate # _____, ground and flight instruction required by FAR 61 Subpart E and find him/her proficient in cross-country flying in a (aircraft make & model)."

For a flight instructor certificate **without** an expiration date:
[date] /s/ J. J. Jones 987654321CFI REED 12-31-2026

For a flight instructor certificate **with** an expiration date:
[date] /s/ J. J. Jones 987654321CFI Exp. 01-31-2025

CFI NOTES:

The authorized instructor who provided the training must make this endorsement.

See cross-country training requirements in subpart E (FAR 61.109) appropriate to the aircraft rating held.

This logbook endorsement MUST be in the pilots' possession or readily accessible in the aircraft when they fly.

RECREATIONAL PILOT WITH FEWER THAN 400 LOGGED FLIGHT HOURS WHO HAS NOT LOGGED PIC TIME WITHIN THE PRECEDING 180 DAYS (REC. PILOT FLIGHT REVIEW')

FAR 61.101 (g)

"I certify I have given Mr./Ms. _____, certificate # _____, flight training required by FAR 61.101 (g) and certify that he/she is proficient to act as pilot in command in a (aircraft make and model)."

For a flight instructor certificate **without** an expiration date:
[date] /s/ J. J. Jones 987654321CFI REED 12-31-2026

For a flight instructor certificate **with** an expiration date:
[date] /s/ J. J. Jones 987654321CFI Exp. 01-31-2025

CFI NOTES:

This endorsement requirement can be made in combination with those required by FAR 61.56 and FAR 61.57 at the discretion of the authorized instructor.

RECREATIONAL PILOT CONDUCTING SOLO FLIGHT FOR THE PURPOSE OF OBTAINING AN ADDITIONAL CERTIFICATE OR RATING WHILE UNDER THE SUPERVISION OF AN AUTHORIZED INSTRUCTOR

FAR 61.101 (i)

"I certify I have given Mr./Ms. _____, certificate # _____, ground and flight instruction required by FAR 61.87 in a (aircraft make and model) and find he/she meets the requirements of the applicable parts of FAR 61.87 and is competent to conduct solo flight in a (aircraft make and model) under the following conditions: (Wind direction & velocity, crosswind component, & weather limitations)."

For a flight instructor certificate **without** an expiration date:
[date] /s/ J. J. Jones 987654321CFI REED 12-31-2026

For a flight instructor certificate **with** an expiration date:
[date] /s/ J. J. Jones 987654321CFI Exp. 01-31-2025

CFI NOTES:
The authorized instructor who provided the training must make this endorsement AND this endorsement MUST be made for EACH flight.

List all conditions that would require the endorsement:
- *Aircraft category/class which the pilot does not hold an appropriate rating.*
- *Within airspace which requires communication with ATC.*
- *Flight between sunset and sunrise provided flight or ground visibility exceeds 5 statute miles.*

FAR 61.87 lists the Solo Requirements for Student Pilots.
The Recreational Pilot may ONLY fly solo while this training is being undertaken.

OPERATIONS ASPIC IN CLASS B/C/D AIRSPACE & AT AN AIRPORT IN CLASS B/C/D/ AIRSPACE
FAR 61.101 (d)

"I certify that I have given Mr./Ms. _____, certificate # _____, the ground and flight instruction required by FAR 61.101 (d) and find him/her proficient in the aeronautical knowledge areas stipulated and to act as PIC in (specific name) Class (B/C/D) airspace and (specific name) airport."

For a flight instructor certificate **without** an expiration date:
[date] /s/ J. J. Jones 987654321CFI REED 12-31-2026

For a flight instructor certificate **with** an expiration date:
[date] /s/ J. J. Jones 987654321CFI Exp. 01-31-2025

CFI NOTES:

The authorized instructor who provided the training must make this endorsement.

This logbook endorsement MUST be in the pilots' possession or readily accessible in the aircraft when they fly.

FAR 91, Appendix D, Section 4 lists those airports at which Recreational Pilot activity is prohibited.

NOTES:

SPORT PILOT

SPORT PILOT AERONAUTICAL KNOWLEDGE
FAR 61.35 (a)(l) & 61.307 (a)

"I certify that I have given Mr./Ms. _____, certificate # _____, the flight and ground instruction on those subject areas listed in FAR 61.309 and have determined he/she is prepared for the Sport Pilot Knowledge Test."

For a flight instructor certificate **without** an expiration date:
[date] /s/ J. J. Jones 987654321CFI REED 12-31-2026

For a flight instructor certificate **with** an expiration date:
[date] /s/ J. J. Jones 987654321CFI Exp. 01-31-2025

OR: If the applicant has completed a home study course:

"I have reviewed the (specific name) home study course work of Mr./Ms._____, and have determined the requirements of FAR 61.309 have been met and he/she is prepared for the Sport Pilot Knowledge Test."

For a flight instructor certificate **without** an expiration date:
[date] /s/ J. J. Jones 987654321CFI REED 12-31-2026

For a flight instructor certificate **with** an expiration date:
[date] /s/ J. J. Jones 987654321CFI Exp. 01-31-2025

CFI NOTES:

The authorized instructor who provided the training or reviewed the home study course materials must make this endorsement.

This endorsement may be made by either a CFI or a CFI-Sport Pilot.

SPORT PILOT FLIGHT PROFICIENCY
FAR 61.39 (a)(6) & 61.307 (b)

"I certify I have given Mr./Ms. _____(Student Pilot certificate #) flight instruction required by FAR 61.311 and find he/she meets the applicable aeronautical knowledge and appropriate flight experience requirements and is prepared for the (*) Sport Pilot Practical Test."

For a flight instructor certificate **without** an expiration date:
[date] /s/ J. J. Jones 987654321CFI REED 12-31-2026

For a flight instructor certificate **with** an expiration date:
[date] /s/ J. J. Jones 987654321CFI Exp. 01-31-2025

CFI NOTES:

- *Insert as appropriate:*
- *Airplane single-engine land/sea*
- *Glider*
- *Gyroplane*
- *Airship*
- *Balloon*
- *Powered Parachute land/sea*
- *Weight-shift control land/sea*

Assure the endorsement for instruction within two calendar months for the practical test (Sport Pilot 7) is accomplished.

This endorsement may be made by either a CFI or a CFI-Sport Pilot.

SPORT PILOT ADDITIONAL CATEGORY/CLASS
FAR61.321

"I certify I have given Mr./Ms. _____, certificate # _____, the additional knowledge and flight training required by FAR 61.309 and 61.311 and he/she meets those requirements for (*) Sport Pilot."

For a flight instructor certificate **without** an expiration date:
[date] /s/ J. J. Jones 987654321CFI REED 12-31-2026

For a flight instructor certificate **with** an expiration date:
[date] /s/ J. J. Jones 987654321CFI Exp. 01-31-2025

CFI NOTES:

- *Insert as appropriate:*
- *Airplane single-engine land/sea*
- *Glider*
- *Gyroplane*
- *Airship*
- *Balloon*
- *Powered Parachute land/sea*
- *Weight-shift control land/sea*

The authorized instructor who provided the training must make this endorsement.

This endorsement may be made by either a CFI or a CFI-Sport Pilot.

The Proficiency Check required by this section and the endorsement above may be made by an authorized instructor other than the instructor who provided the original training.

SPORT PILOT ADDITIONAL MAKE/MODEL WITHIN SAME CATEGORY &/OR CLASS
FAR61.323

"I certify that I have given Mr./Ms. _____, certificate # _____, additional aeronautical knowledge and flight instruction required by FAR 61.309 and 61.311 and find him/her proficient to operate a (make and model) light-sport aircraft."

For a flight instructor certificate **without** an expiration date:
[date] /s/ J. J. Jones 987654321CFI REED 12-31-2026

For a flight instructor certificate **with** an expiration date:
[date] /s/ J. J. Jones 987654321CFI Exp. 01-31-2025

CFI NOTES:

The authorized instructor 1vho provided the training must make this endorsement.

This endorsement may be made by either a CFI or a CFI-Sport Pilot

OPERATION OF LIGHT-SPORT AIRCRAFT WITHIN CLASS B/C/D AIRSPACE AND/OR AT CLASS B/C/D AIRPORTS
FAR 61.325 (a - c)

"I certify that I have given Mr./Ms. _____, certificate # _____, aeronautical knowledge and flight instruction required by FAR 61.325 (a - c) and find him/her proficient to operate [within Class (*) airspace] or [at Class (*) airports]."

For a flight instructor certificate **without** an expiration date:
[date] /s/ J. J. Jones 987654321CFI REED 12-31-2026

For a flight instructor certificate **with** an expiration date:
[date] /s/ J. J. Jones 987654321CFI Exp. 01-31-2025

CFI NOTES:

* Insert as appropriate: specific name B/C/D

The authorized instructor who provided this training must make this endorsement.

This endorsement may be made by either a CFI or a CFI-Sport Pilot.

FAR 91, Appendix D, Section 4 lists those airports at which Sport Pilot activity is prohibited.

OPERATION OF LIGHT-SPORT AIRCRAFT WITH Vh GREATER THAN 87 kts CAS
FAR61.327

"I certify that I have given Mr./Ms. _____, certificate # _____, ground and flight instruction required by FAR 61.327 and find him/her proficient to operate a light-sport aircraft with a Vh greater than 87 kts CAS."

For a flight instructor certificate **without** an expiration date:
[date] /s/ J. J. Jones 987654321CFI REED 12-31-2026

For a flight instructor certificate **with** an expiration date:
[date] /s/ J. J. Jones 987654321CFI Exp. 01-31-2025

CFI NOTES:

The authorized instructor who provided the training must make this endorsement.

This endorsement may be made by either a CFI or a CFI-Sport Pilot.

PREREQUISITES FOR PRACTICAL TEST
FAR 61.39(a)(6)

"I certify that I have given Mr./Ms. _____, certificate # _____, training within the preceding two calendar months and he/she is prepared for the test. He/she has also demonstrated satisfactory knowledge of the subject areas found deficient on the Airman's Knowledge Test."

For a flight instructor certificate **without** an expiration date:
[date] /s/ J. J. Jones 987654321CFI REED 12-31-2026

For a flight instructor certificate **with** an expiration date:
[date] /s/ J. J. Jones 987654321CFI Exp. 01-31-2025

CFI NOTES:

The authorized instructor who provided the training must make this endorsement.

This endorsement may be made by either a CFI or a CFI-Sport Pilot.

SPORT PILOT
FLIGHT
INSTRUCTOR

SPORT PILOT FLIGHT INSTRUCTOR AERONAUTICAL KNOWLEDGE
FAR 61.35 (a)(l) & 61.405 (a)

"I certify I have given Mr./Ms. _____ certificate # _____, ground instruction required by FAR 407 (*) and that he/she is prepared for the Flight Instructor Sport Pilot (Knowledge/POI) Test."

For a flight instructor certificate **without** an expiration date:
[date] /s/ J. J. Jones 987654321CFI REED 12-31-2026

For a flight instructor certificate **with** an expiration date:
[date] /s/ J. J. Jones 987654321CFI Exp. 01-31-2025

OR: If a home study course:

"I have reviewed the (specific name) home study course work of Mr./Ms. _____, certificate # _____, and have determined he/she is prepared for the Flight Instructor Sport Pilot (Knowledge/POI) Test."

For a flight instructor certificate **without** an expiration date:
[date] /s/ J. J. Jones 987654321CFI REED 12-31-2026

For a flight instructor certificate **with** an expiration date:
[date] /s/ J. J. Jones 987654321CFI Exp. 01-31-2025

CFI NOTES:
Insert as appropriate:
   For FOI Knowledge test-FAR 61.407(a). This test is unnecessary if the applicant meets the requirements of FAR 61.407(c)
   For CFI-SP Aeronautical Knowledge test-FAR 61.407(b)
The authorized instructor who provided the training or reviewed the home-study course must make this endorsement.
This endorsement may be made by either a CFI or a CFI-Sport Pilot.

SPORT PILOT FLIGHT INSTRUCTOR FLIGHT PROFICIENCY
FAR 61.39 (a)(6) & 61.405 (b)(l)(i)

"I certify that I have given Mr./Ms. _____, certificate # _____, ground and flight instruction required by FAR 61.409 and find him/her prepared for the Sport Pilot Flight Instructor Practical Test."

For a flight instructor certificate **without** an expiration date:
[date] /s/ J. J. Jones 987654321CFI REED 12-31-2026

For a flight instructor certificate **with** an expiration date:
[date] /s/ J. J. Jones 987654321CFI Exp. 01-31-2025

CFI NOTES:

The authorized instructor who provided the training must make this endorsement.

This endorsement may be made by either a CFI or a CFI-Sport Pilot.

Assure the Prerequisites for Practical Test endorsement (Sport Pilot 7) is accomplished as well.

SPORT PILOT FLIGHT INSTRUCTOR SPIN PROFICIENCY
FAR 61.405 (b)(l)(ii)

"I certify that I have given Mr./Ms. _____, certificate # _____, ground and flight instruction required by FAR 61.405 (b)(l)(ii) in stall awareness, spin entry, spins, and spin recovery procedures and find him/her competent and possessing instructional proficiency in those manoeuvres."

For a flight instructor certificate **without** an expiration date:
[date] /s/ J. J. Jones 987654321CFI REED 12-31-2026

For a flight instructor certificate **with** an expiration date:
[date] /s/ J. J. Jones 987654321CFI Exp. 01-31-2025

CFI NOTES:

This endorsement is required for Airplane and Glider candidates ONLY and must be accomplished in an aircraft certificated for spins.

This endorsement may be made by either a CFI or a CFI-Sport Pilot.

The authorized instructor who provided this training must make this endorsement.

An examiner MAY accept this endorsement as satisfactory evidence of instructional proficiency; however, if the applicant scares the examiner during these maneuvers (a for-sure bust) AND/OR the flightcheck is a retest due to failure to demonstrate instructional proficiency, these maneuvers WILL be retested and evaluated critically.

SPORT PILOT FLIGHT INSTRUCTOR
ADDITIONAL CATEGORY/CLASS
FAR 61.419 (a)

"I certify that I have given Mr./Ms. _____, certificate # _____, training required by FAR 61.409 and find him/her proficient to add (category/class) aircraft to his/her Light-sport Flight Instructor certificate."

For a flight instructor certificate **without** an expiration date:
[date] /s/ J. J. Jones 987654321CFI REED 12-31-2026

For a flight instructor certificate **with** an expiration date:
[date] /s/ J. J. Jones 987654321CFI Exp. 01-31-2025

CFI NOTES:

The authorized instructor who provided this training must make this endorsement.

This endorsement may be made by either a CFI or a CFI-Sport Pilot.

The Proficiency Check required by FAR 61.419(b) and this endorsement may be made by an authorized instructor other than the instructor who provided the original training.

NOTES:

PRIVATE PILOT

PRIVATE PILOT AERONAUTICAL KNOWLEDGE
FAR 61.35 (a)(l) & 61.103 (d)

"I certify that I have given Mr./Ms. _____, certificate # _____, ground instruction required by FAR 61.105 (b) and he/she is prepared for the Private Pilot Knowledge Test."

For a flight instructor certificate **without** an expiration date:
[date] /s/ J. J. Jones 987654321CFI REED 12-31-2026

For a flight instructor certificate **with** an expiration date:
[date] /s/ J. J. Jones 987654321CFI Exp. 01-31-2025

OR if student has completed a home study course:

"I have reviewed the (specific name) home study course work of Mr./Ms. _____, certificate # _____, and have determined the requirements of FAR 61.105 (b) have been met and he/she is prepared for the Private Pilot Knowledge Test."

For a flight instructor certificate **without** an expiration date:
[date] /s/ J. J. Jones 987654321CFI REED 12-31-2026

For a flight instructor certificate **with** an expiration date:
[date] /s/ J. J. Jones 987654321CFI Exp. 01-31-2025

CFI NOTES:

The authorized instructor who provided the training or reviewed the home- study course should make either endorsement.

PRIVATE PILOT FLIGHT PROFICIENCY
FAR 61.103 (t)

"I certify that I have given Mr./Ms. _____, certificate # _____, the flight instruction required by FAR 61.107 (b) ( ) and find him/her prepared to perform each pilot operation safely as a Private Pilot."

For a flight instructor certificate **without** an expiration date:
[date] /s/ J. J. Jones 987654321CFI REED 12-31-2026

For a flight instructor certificate **with** an expiration date:
[date] /s/ J. J. Jones 987654321CFI Exp. 01-31-2025

CFI NOTES:

* FAR 61.107 (b) sub-sections are:

> *(1) Airplane single-engine*
> *(2) Airplane multi-engine*
> *(3) Rotorcraft helicopter*
> *(4) Rotorcraft gyroplane*
> *(5) Powered-lift*
> *(6) Glider*
> *(7) Lighter than air airship*
> *(8) Lighter than air balloon*
> *(9) Powered parachute*
> *(10) Weight-shift control aircraft*

The authorized instructor who provided the training must make this endorsement

PREREQUISITES FOR PRACTICAL TESTS
FAR 61.39 (a)(6)

"I certify that I have given Mr./Ms. _____, certificate # _____, flight instruction required by FAR 61.39(a)(6) within the preceding two calendar months and find him/her prepared for the exam. He/she has demonstrated satisfactory knowledge of the subject areas shown to be deficient on his/her Airman Knowledge Test."

For a flight instructor certificate **without** an expiration date:
[date] /s/ J. J. Jones 987654321CFI REED 12-31-2026

For a flight instructor certificate **with** an expiration date:
[date] /s/ J. J. Jones 987654321CFI Exp. 01-31-2025

CFI NOTES:
The authorized instructor who provided the training must make this endorsement.
Private Pilot endorsements 2 & 3 may be combined to read:
"I certify I have given Mr./Ms. _____, certificate # _____, the flight instruction required by FAR 61.107(b)(*) & FAR 61.39(a)(6) within the preceding two calendar months and find him/her prepared to perform each pilot operation safely as a Private Pilot. He/she has demonstrated satisfactory knowledge of the subject areas shown to be deficient on his/her Airman Knowledge Test."

*For a flight instructor certificate **without** an expiration date:*
[date] /s/ J. J. Jones 987654321CFI REED 12-31-2026

*For a flight instructor certificate **with** an expiration date:*
[date] /s/ J. J. Jones 987654321CFI Exp. 01-31-2025

* FAR 61.107 (b) sub-sections are:

1.Airplane single-engine
2. Airplane multi-engine
3. Rotorcraft helicopter
4. Rotorcraft gyroplane
5. Powered-lift
6. Glider

7. Lighter than air airship
8. Lighter than air balloon
9. Powered parachute
10. Weight-shift control aircraft

COMMERCIAL
PILOT

COMMERCIAL PILOT AERONAUTICAL KNOWLEDGE
FAR 61.35 (a)(l) & 61.123 (c)

"I certify I have given Mr./Ms. _____, certificate # _____, ground instruction required by FAR 61.125 (b) and he/she is prepared for the Commercial Pilot Knowledge Test."

For a flight instructor certificate **without** an expiration date:
[date] /s/ J. J. Jones 987654321CFI REED 12-31-2026

For a flight instructor certificate **with** an expiration date:
[date] /s/ J. J. Jones 987654321CFI Exp. 01-31-2025

OR if student has completed a home study course:

"I certify that I have reviewed the (specific name) home study course work of Mr./Ms. _____, certificate #_____,and determine the requirements of FAR 61.125 (b) have been met and that he/she is prepared for the Commercial Pilot Knowledge Test."

For a flight instructor certificate **without** an expiration date:
[date] /s/ J. J. Jones 987654321CFI REED 12-31-2026

For a flight instructor certificate **with** an expiration date:
[date] /s/ J. J. Jones 987654321CFI Exp. 01-31-2025

CFI NOTES:

The authorized instructor who provided the training or reviewed the home study course should make either endorsement.

COMMERCIAL PILOT FLIGHT PROFICIENCY
FAR 61.123 (e)

"I certify I have given Mr./Ms. _____, certificate # _____, the flight training required by FAR 61.127 (b) (*) and find him/her prepared to perform each pilot operation safely as a Commercial Pilot."

For a flight instructor certificate **without** an expiration date:
[date] /s/ J. J. Jones 987654321CFI REED 12-31-2026

For a flight instructor certificate **with** an expiration date:
[date] /s/ J. J. Jones 987654321CFI Exp. 01-31-2025

CFI NOTES:

* FAR 61.127 (b) sub-sections are:
> *(1) Airplane single-engine*
> *(2) Airplane multi-engine*
> *(3) Rotorcraft helicopter*
> *(4) Rotorcraft gyroplane*
> *(5) Powered-lift*
> *(6) Glider*
> *(7) Lighter-than-air airship*
> *(8) Lighter-than-air balloon*

PREREQUISITES FOR PRACTICAL TESTS
FAR 61.39 (a)(6)

"I certify I have given Mr./Ms. _____, certificate # _____, the flight instruction required by FAR 61.39 (a)(6) within the preceding two calendar and find him/her prepared for the exam. He/she has demonstrated satisfactory knowledge of the subject areas shown to be deficient on his/her Airman Knowledge Test."

For a flight instructor certificate **without** an expiration date:
[date] /s/ J. J. Jones 987654321CFI REED 12-31-2026

For a flight instructor certificate **with** an expiration date:
[date] /s/ J. J. Jones 987654321CFI Exp. 01-31-2025

CFI NOTES:

Commercial Pilot endorsements 2 & 3 may be combined to read:

"I certify I have given Mr./Ms._____, certificate # _____, flight training required by FAR 61.127(b)(*) & FAR 61.39(a)(6) within the preceding two calendar months and find him/her prepared to perform each pilot operation safely as a Commercial Pilot. He/she has demonstrated satisfactory knowledge of the subject areas shown to be deficient on his/her Airman Knowledge Test."

The authorized instructor who provided the training must make this endorsement.
* FAR 61.127 (b) sub-sections are:

1. Airplane single-engine
2. Airplane multi-engine
3. Rotorcraft helicopter
4. Rotorcraft gyroplane
5. Powered-lift

6. Glider
7. Lighter-than-air airship
8. Lighter-than-air balloon

AIRLINE
TRANSPORT
PILOT

PREREQUISITES FOR PRACTICAL TESTS
FAR 61.39 (a) (6)

"I certify I have determined Mr./Ms._____, certificate # _____, the flight instruction required by FAR 61.39(a) (6) within the preceding two calendar months and find him/her prepared for the exam. He/she has demonstrated satisfactory knowledge of the subject areas shown to be deficient on his/her Airman Knowledge Test."

For a flight instructor certificate **without** an expiration date:
[date] /s/ J. J. Jones 987654321CFI REED 12-31-2026

For a flight instructor certificate **with** an expiration date:
[date] /s/ J. J. Jones 987654321CFI Exp. 01-31-2025

CFI NOTES:

Exceptions to the requirements of this FAR are listed in FAR 61.157(c)

TYPE RATING ADDED TO EXISTING ATP CERTIFICATE
FAR 61.157(b)

"I certify I have determined Mr./Ms._____,
certificate # _____, the required training required
by FAR 61.157 (e) (*) in those areas of operation applicable to the
addition of a (aircraft type) type rating to his/her existing ATP
certificate."

For a flight instructor certificate **without** an expiration date:
[date] /s/ J. J. Jones 987654321CFI REED 12-31-2026

For a flight instructor certificate **with** an expiration date:
[date] /s/ J. J. Jones 987654321CFI Exp. 01-31-2025

CFI NOTES:

* FAR 61.157(e) sub-sections are:
(1) Airplane single-engine
(2) Airplane multi-engine
(3) Powered lift
(4) Rotorcraft helicopter

*Exceptions to this rule (employee of a Part 121 or 135
certificate holder) are listed in FAR 61.157(c)*

*Proficiency & competency checks conducted under applicable
FARs listed in FAR 61.157(f) satisfy the flight proficiency
requirements for an ATP certificate and/ or appropriate type rating.*

NOTES:

FLIGHT INSTRUCTOR AERONAUTICAL KNOWLEDGE
FAR 61.35 (a)(l) & 61.183 (d)

"I certify I have (either a or b)
    a. given Mr./Ms._____, certificate # _____, the
    required ground instruction required by:
        •(for FOI Knowledge) FAR 61.185 (a)(l)
        •(for CFI-A Knowledge) FAR 61.185 (a)(2)
        •(for CFI-IA Knowledge) FAR 61.185 (a)(3)
    b. reviewed the home study course materials

and he/she is prepared for the (<u>specific name</u>) Knowledge Test."

For a flight instructor certificate **without** an expiration date:
[date] /s/ J. J. Jones 987654321CFI REED 12-31-2026

For a flight instructor certificate **with** an expiration date:
[date] /s/ J. J. Jones 987654321CFI Exp. 01-31-2025

CFI NOTES:

As of 1 September 2024, ALL flight instructor candidates MUST have written (or electronic) endorsements shown above in their logbook or training record for ALL knowledge tests.
The endorsements in this section are for OTHER than Sport Pilot Fight Instructors. See the Sport Pilot Flight Instructor section of this book for CFI-Sport Pilot endorsements.

FLIGHT INSTRUCTOR FLIGHT PROFICIENCY
FAR 61.183 (g) & FAR 61.187 (a)

"I certify I have determined Mr./Ms._____,
certificate # _____, flight instruction
required by FAR 61.187 (b) (*) and find him/her proficient to
pass the Flight Instructor practical test."

For a flight instructor certificate **without** an expiration date:
[date] /s/ J. J. Jones 987654321CFI REED 12-31-2026

For a flight instructor certificate **with** an expiration date:
[date] /s/ J. J. Jones 987654321CFI Exp. 01-31-2025

CFI NOTES:

* FAR 61.187 (b) sub-sections are:
  (1) Airplane single-engine
  (2) Airplane multi-engine
  (3) Rotorcraft helicopter
  (4) Rotorcraft gyroplane
  (5) Powered-lift
  (6) Glider
  *(7) Instrument instructor with appropriate aircraft category and
    class rating (requires CFII to make the endorsement)*

*This endorsement must be made by an appropriately-rated
authorized Flight Instructor (e.g. CFI-ME, CFI-H, etc.) who
provided the training.*

*To train INITIAL CFI candidates, the authorized instructor must
meet the requirements of FAR 61.195(h)*

FLIGHT INSTRUCTOR SPIN PROFICIENCY
FAR 61.183 (i)(l)

"I certify I have determined Mr./Ms._____, certificate # _____, ground and flight training required by FAR 61.183 (i)(l) in stall awareness, spin entry, spins and spin recovery procedures and find he/she has demonstrated instructional proficiency in those manoeuvres."

For a flight instructor certificate **without** an expiration date:
[date] /s/ J. J. Jones 987654321CFI REED 12-31-2026

For a flight instructor certificate **with** an expiration date:
[date] /s/ J. J. Jones 987654321CFI Exp. 01-31-2025

CFI NOTES:

The above endorsement is required only of Flight Instructor - Airplane and Flight Instructor - Glider candidates.

The airplane or glider used MUST be certificated for spins.

An examiner MAY accept this endorsement as satisfactory evidence of instructional proficiency; however, if the applicant scares the examiner during these maneuvers (a for-sure bust) AND/OR the flightcheck is a retest due to failure to demonstrate instructional proficiency, these maneuvers WILL be retested and evaluated critically.

AUTHORITY TO PROVIDE NIGHT-VISION GOGGLES TRAINING
FAR 61.195 (k)

"I certify I have determined Mr./Ms._____, certificate # _____, meets the requirements of FAR 61.195 (k)(1-6) and is qualified to conduct training in night-vision goggle operations."

For a flight instructor certificate **without** an expiration date:
[date] /s/ J. J. Jones 987654321CFI REED 12-31-2026

For a flight instructor certificate **with** an expiration date:
[date] /s/ J. J. Jones 987654321CFI Exp. 01-31-2025

CFI NOTES:

Specific requirements listed in FAR 61.195(k) must be met in order to receive this endorsement.

Only an FAA inspector or person specifically authorized by the FAA to provide this endorsement may make this endorsement (FAR 61.195(k) (7)

PREREQUISITES FOR PRACTICAL TESTS
FAR 61.39 (a)(6)

"I certify I have given Mr./Ms._____, certificate # _____, flight instruction required by FAR 61.39 (a) 6 within the preceding two calendar months and find him/her prepared for the exam. He/she has demonstrated satisfactory knowledge of the subject areas shown to be deficient on his/her Airman Knowledge Test."

For a flight instructor certificate **without** an expiration date:
[date] /s/ J. J. Jones 987654321CFI REED 12-31-2026

For a flight instructor certificate **with** an expiration date:
[date] /s/ J. J. Jones 987654321CFI Exp. 01-31-2025

CFI NOTES:
CFI endorsements 2 & 5 may be combined to read:
"I certify I have given Mr./Ms._____, certificate # _____, flight instruction required by FAR 61.187(b)(*) & FAR61.39 (a)(6) within the preceding two calendar months and find him/her proficient to pass the Flight Instructor practical test. He/she has demonstrated satisfactory knowledge of the subject areas shown to be deficient on his/her Airman Knowledge Test."

*For a flight instructor certificate **without** an expiration date:*
[date] /s/ J. J. Jones 987654321CFI REED 12-31-2026

*For a flight instructor certificate **with** an expiration date:*
[date] /s/ J. J. Jones 987654321CFI Exp. 01-31-2025

* .FAR 61.187(b) sub-sections are:

(1) Airplane single-engine	*(6) Glider*
(2) Airplane multi-engine	*(7) Instrument instructor with*
(3) Rotorcraft helicopter	*appropriate aircraft category and class*
(4) Rotorcraft gyroplane	*rating (requires CFII to make the*
(5) Powered-lift	*endorsement)*

This endorsement must be made by an appropriately-rated authorized Flight Instructor (e.g. CFI-ME, CFI-H, etc.) who gave the training. To train INITIAL CFI candidates, the authorized instructor must meet the requirements of FAR 61.195(h)

INSTRUMENT RATING

SPRINGS TOWER,

"Roger. Understand cleared for a straight in approach."

INSTRUMENT PILOT AERONAUTICAL KNOWLEDGE
FAR 61.35 (a)(l) & 61.65 (a)(4)

"I certify that I have given Mr./Ms. _____, certificate # _____, ground instruction required by FAR 61.65 (b) and he/she is prepared for the Instrument Rating Knowledge Test."

For a flight instructor certificate **without** an expiration date:
[date] /s/ J. J. Jones 987654321CFI REED 12-31-2026

For a flight instructor certificate **with** an expiration date:
[date] /s/ J. J. Jones 987654321CFI Exp. 01-31-2025

OR: if student has completed a home study course:

"I have reviewed the (specific name) home study course work of Mr./Ms._____, certificate # _____, and have determined the requirements of FAR 61.65 (a)(4) have been met and he/she is prepared for the Instrument Rating Knowledge Test."

For a flight instructor certificate **without** an expiration date:
[date] /s/ J. J. Jones 987654321CFI REED 12-31-2026

For a flight instructor certificate **with** an expiration date:
[date] /s/ J. J. Jones 987654321CFI Exp. 01-31-2025

CFI-IA NOTES:

The authorized instructor who provided the training or reviewed the home- study course should make either endorsement.

INSTRUMENT RATING FLIGHT PROFICIENCY
FAR 61.39 (a)(6) & 61.65 (a)(6)

"I certify I have given Mr./Ms._____, certificate # _____,instrument flight instruction required by FAR 61.65 (c) and find him/her prepared to take the Instrument Rated Practical Test."

For a flight instructor certificate **without** an expiration date:
[date] /s/ J. J. Jones 987654321CFI REED 12-31-2026

For a flight instructor certificate **with** an expiration date:
[date] /s/ J. J. Jones 987654321CFI Exp. 01-31-2025

CFI-IA NOTES:

The authorized instructor who provided the training must make this endorsement.

Use of a Flight Simulator or Flight Training Device for the Flight Check is detailed in FAR 61.65(a)(8).

PREREQUISITES FOR PRACTICAL TESTS
FAR 61.39 (a)(6)

"I certify I have given Mr./Ms._____, certificate # _____, the flight instruction required by FAR 61.39 (a)(6) within the preceding two calendar months and find him/her prepared for the exam. He/she has demonstrated satisfactory knowledge of the subject areas shown to be deficient on his/her Airman Knowledge Test."

For a flight instructor certificate **without** an expiration date:
[date] /s/ J. J. Jones 987654321CFI REED 12-31-2026

For a flight instructor certificate **with** an expiration date:
[date] /s/ J. J. Jones 987654321CFI Exp. 01-31-2025

CFI- IA NOTES:
Instrument rating endorsements 2 & 3 may be combined to read:
"I certify I have given Mr./Ms._____, certificate #_____, the instrument flight training required by FAR 61.39 (a)(6) & FAR 61.65 (a) (6) within the preceding two calendar months and find him/ her prepared to take the Instrument Rating practical test. He/she has demonstrated satisfactory knowledge of the subject areas shown to be deficient on his/her airman knowledge test."

For a flight instructor certificate **without** an expiration date:
[date] /s/ J. J. Jones 987654321CFI REED 12-31-2026

For a flight instructor certificate **with** an expiration date:
[date] /s/ J. J. Jones 987654321CFI Exp. 01-31-2025

The authorized instructor who provided the training must make this endorsement.

MULTI-ENGINE RATING

ADDITIONAL CLASS RATING FLIGHT PROFICIENCY
FAR 61.63 (c)

"I certify I have given Mr./Ms_____, certificate # _____, the ground and flight instruction required by FAR 61.63(c) and find him/her competent in the appropriate aeronautical knowledge areas of, and proficient in, the appropriate areas of operation for the (Private/Commercial) pilot practical test for the addition of an Airplane Multi-engine (Land/Sea) rating."

For a flight instructor certificate **without** an expiration date:
[date] /s/ J. J. Jones 987654321CFI REED 12-31-2026

For a flight instructor certificate **with** an expiration date:
[date] /s/ J. J. Jones 987654321CFI Exp. 01-31-2025

CFI-ME NOTES:

This endorsement is used on other than ATP certificates.

The authorized instructor who provided the training must make this endorsement.

PREREQUISITES FOR PRACTICAL TESTS
FAR 61.39 (a)(6)

"I certify I have given Mr./Ms. _____certificate # _____,the flight instruction required by FAR 61.39 (a)(6) within the preceding two calendar months and find him/her prepared for the exam."

For a flight instructor certificate **without** an expiration date:
[date] /s/ J. J. Jones 987654321CFI REED 12-31-2026

For a flight instructor certificate **with** an expiration date:
[date] /s/ J. J. Jones 987654321CFI Exp. 01-31-2025

CFI-ME NOTES:

Multi-engine endorsements 1 & 2 may be combined to read:

"I certify I have given Mr./Ms_____, certificate #_____, the ground and flight instruction required by FAR 61.63 (c) & FAR 61.39 (a)(6) within the preceding two calendar months and find him/her prepared to pass the (Private / Commercial) pilot practical test for the addition of an Airplane Multi-engine (Land/Sea) rating."

*For a flight instructor certificate **without** an expiration date:
[date] /s/ J. J. Jones 987654321CFI REED 12-31-2026*

*For a flight instructor certificate **with** an expiration date:
[date] /s/ J. J. Jones 987654321CFI Exp. 01-31-2025*

The authorized instructor who provided the training must make this endorsement

NOTES:

MISCELLANEOUS
ENDORSEMENTS

FLIGHT REVIEW
FAR 61.56 (c)

"I certify I have given Mr./Ms._____, certificate # _____, as satisfactorily completed the Flight Review required by FAR 61.56 (c) on (Date)."

For a flight instructor certificate **without** an expiration date:
[date] /s/ J. J. Jones 987654321CFI REED 12-31-2026

For a flight instructor certificate **with** an expiration date:
[date] /s/ J. J. Jones 987654321CFI Exp. 01-31-2025

CFI NOTES:

The authorized instructor who administered the review must make this endorsement.

Unsatisfactory performance on a BFR does not require a written logbook entry reflecting failure; a logbook entry indicating 'dual received' is sufficient until the applicant can meet the appropriate standards of knowledge and/or performance.

Passing a pilot proficiency check for a pilot certificate, rating or operating privilege, or accomplishing one or more phases of an FAA-sponsored pilot proficiency award (Wings) program, will fulfill the requirement(s) for a flight review. Ask the examiner to make the appropriate endorsement in your logbook.

A Flight Simulator or Flight Training Device may be used only IF the requirements of FAR 61.56(i)(1-3) are met.

FAR 61.56(1) A Flight Instructor who has renewed their flight instructor certificate need not accomplish the 1 hour of ground instruction requirement.

FLIGHT REVIEW ACCOMPLISHED via the PILOT PROFICIENCY or "WINGS" PROGRAM
FAR 61.56 (e)

"I certify I have given Mr./Ms. _____ certificate # _____, has satisfactorily completed a Flight Review required by FAR 61.56 (e) under the Pilot Proficiency Program."

For a flight instructor certificate **without** an expiration date:
[date] /s/ J. J. Jones 987654321CFI REED 12-31-2026

For a flight instructor certificate **with** an expiration date:
[date] /s/ J. J. Jones 987654321CFI Exp. 01-31-2025

CFI NOTES:

A pilot who has successfully completed a phase of the "Wings" program is exempted from undertaking the one (1) hour flight requirement per FAR 61.56(c)(1)(2)

When a pilot has documentation proving completion of a phase of the Pilot Proficiency program, an authorized instructor may enter this endorsement in the pilot's logbook.

All CFI's are encouraged to participate in the FAA Pilot Proficiency program by registering themselves - and encouraging their students and clients to register - at: www.FAASafety.gov

You, your students and clients will be electronically notified of upcoming safety seminars, events and information regarding Aviation Safety.

Pilots will find online classes that will qualify for all phases of the Pilot Proficiency program.

INSTRUMENT PROFICIENCY CHECK
FAR 61.57 (d)

"I certify I have given Mr./Ms._____, certificate # _____, has satisfactorily completed an Instrument Proficiency Check as prescribed in FAR 61.57 (d) on (Date)."

For a flight instructor certificate **without** an expiration date:
[date] /s/ J. J. Jones 987654321CFI REED 12-31-2026

For a flight instructor certificate **with** an expiration date:
[date] /s/ J. J. Jones 987654321CFI Exp. 01-31-2025

CFI-IA NOTES:

The authorized instructor who administered the PC must make this endorsement.

The Instrument Proficiency Check must consist of the areas of operation and instrument tasks listed on the appropriate table in the Instrument Rating Practical Test Standards.

This endorsement is intended for the pilot who is not current on instruments to regain currency and begin anew the six months instrument proficiency cycle.

Unsatisfactory performance on an IPC does not require a written logbook entry reflecting failure; a logbook entry indicating (dual received) is sufficient. Pilots exempted from the requirement of FAR 61.57 (d) are listed in FAR 61.57 (e)

An IPC may be given in an aircraft appropriate to the aircraft category or for other than a glider in a simulator or flight training device representative of aircraft category and so certified or documented.

INSTRUMENT CURRENCY
FAR 61.57 (c)

"I certify I have given Mr./Ms. _____ certificate # _____, has satisfactorily maintained Instrument Currency required under FAR 61.57 (c)(1) by accomplishing six instrument approaches, holding procedures and intercepting and tracking a course, airway or published route segment."

For a flight instructor certificate **without** an expiration date:
[date] /s/ J. J. Jones 987654321CFI REED 12-31-2026

For a flight instructor certificate **with** an expiration date:
[date] /s/ J. J. Jones 987654321CFI Exp. 01-31-2025

CFI-IA NOTES:

This endorsement is intended for the current instrument pilot who has performed the requisite requirements with their CFI-IA to maintain instrument currency for a new six-month cycle.

COMPLEX AIRCRAFT
FAR 61.31 (e)(l)

"I certify I have given Mr./Ms._____, certificate # _____, ground and flight instruction required by FAR 61.31 (e)(l) and find him/her proficient to operate a complex airplane."

For a flight instructor certificate **without** an expiration date:
[date] /s/ J. J. Jones 987654321CFI REED 12-31-2026

For a flight instructor certificate **with** an expiration date:
[date] /s/ J. J. Jones 987654321CFI Exp. 01-31-2025

CFI NOTES:

Exceptions to the training and endorsement requirements are found in FAR 61.31 (e)(2).

The authorized instructor who provided the training must make this endorsement.

HIGH-PERFORMANCE AIRCRAFT
FAR 61.31 (f)(l)

"I certify I have given Mr./Ms. _____, certificate # _____, ground and flight instruction required by FAR 61.31(f)(!), and find him/her proficient to operate a high-performance airplane."

For a flight instructor certificate **without** an expiration date:
[date] /s/ J. J. Jones 987654321CFI REED 12-31-2026

For a flight instructor certificate **with** an expiration date:
[date] /s/ J. J. Jones 987654321CFI Exp. 01-31-2025

CFI NOTES:

Exceptions to the training and endorsement requirements are found in FAR 61.31(f)(2).

The authorized instructor who provided the training must make this endorsement.

TAILWHEEL AIRCRAFT PIC
FAR 61.31 (i)(l)

"I certify I have given Mr./Ms. _____, certificate # _____, flight training required by FAR 61.31 (i)(l) in normal and crosswind takeoffs and landings, wheel landings (if appropriate) and go-around procedures, and find him/her proficient to operate a tailwheel airplane."

For a flight instructor certificate **without** an expiration date:
[date] /s/ J. J. Jones 987654321CFI REED 12-31-2026

For a flight instructor certificate **with** an expiration date:
[date] /s/ J. J. Jones 987654321CFI Exp. 01-31-2025

CFI NOTES:

Exceptions to the training and endorsement requirements are found in FAR 61.31 (f) (2).

The authorized instructor who provided the training must make this endorsement.

PRESSURIZED A/C OPERATING AT HIGH ALTITUDE
FAR 61.31 (g)(l)(2)

"I certify I have given Mr./Ms. _____, certificate # _____, ground training required by FAR 61.31 (g)(l) and the (flight/simulator/ flight training device) training required by FAR 61.31 (g)(2) and find him/her proficient in the operation of pressurized aircraft."

For a flight instructor certificate **without** an expiration date:
[date] /s/ J. J. Jones 987654321CFI REED 12-31-2026

For a flight instructor certificate **with** an expiration date:
[date] /s/ J. J. Jones 987654321CFI Exp. 01-31-2025

CFI NOTES:

Exceptions to the training and endorsement requirements are found in FAR 61.31 (g)(3).

The authorized instructor who provided the training must make this endorsement.

ADDITIONAL CATEGORY, CLASS or TYPE RATING

FAR 61.3l(d)(2)
FAR 61.63(b) - Additional aircraft category
FAR 61.63(c) - Additional aircraft class
FAR 61.63(d) - Additional type rating
(On other than ATP Certificate)

"I certify I have given Mr./Ms. _____, certificate # _____, instruction required by FAR 61.63 (aircraft make & model) and find him/her competent in the appropriate aeronautical knowledge areas and proficient to pass the (_____) practical test for the addition of a (insert as appropriate) rating."

For a flight instructor certificate **without** an expiration date:
[date] /s/ J. J. Jones 987654321CFI REED 12-31-2026

For a flight instructor certificate **with** an expiration date:
[date] /s/ J. J. Jones 987654321CFI Exp. 01-31-2025

CFI NOTES:
* FAR 61.63 sub-sections are:
>   *(b) Additional aircraft category*
>   *(c) Additional aircraft class*
>   *(d) Additional type rating*

This endorsement should be made when the applicant is adding an additional category, class or type rating to an existing pilot certificate.

Miscellaneous Endorsement 17, instruction within two calendar months prior to a practical test, should be made as well.
This endorsement is for other than ATP certificate.

The authorized instructor who provided the training must make this endorsement.

INITIAL or ADDITIONAL TYPE RATING
FAR 61.63(d)

"I certify I have given Mr./Ms._____, certificate # _____, the ground training required by FAR 61.155(c) & flight training required by FAR 61.157(e) and attest he/she is competent in the appropriate aeronautical knowledge areas and proficient in the appropriate areas of operation at the Airline Transport Pilot certification level."

For a flight instructor certificate **without** an expiration date:
[date] /s/ J. J. Jones 987654321CFI REED 12-31-2026

For a flight instructor certificate **with** an expiration date:
[date] /s/ J. J. Jones 987654321CFI Exp. 01-31-2025

CFI NOTES:

Type ratings may be granted concurrently with the ATP flightcheck by passing the practical test in the same category and class of aircraft for which the applicant holds the type rating(s).

The authorized instructor who provided the training must make this endorsement.

GLIDER & UNPOWERED ULTRALIGHT VEHICLE TOWING
FAR 61.69 (a)(3)

"I certify I have given Mr./Ms. _____, certificate # _____, ground and flight training required by FAR 61.69 (a)(3) and find him/her proficient in the techniques and procedures essential to the safe towing of gliders."

For a flight instructor certificate **without** an expiration date:
[date] /s/ J. J. Jones 987654321CFI REED 12-31-2026

For a flight instructor certificate **with** an expiration date:
[date] /s/ J. J. Jones 987654321CFI Exp. 01-31-2025

CFI-G NOTES:

Qualifications which must be met by those authorized to make this endorsement are detailed in FAR 61.69 (c)

If the pilot being endorsed is a Private Pilot, they must meet the qualifications listed in 61.69 (d)

Training requirements and exceptions are listed throughout FAR 61.69.

The authorized instructor who provided the training must make this endorsement.

FAR 61.69(a)(5)(6) details the currency requirements for a Glider tow pilot.

GLIDER LAUNCH PROCEDURES
FAR 61.31 (j)(l)

"I certify I have given Mr./Ms. _____, certificate # _____, training in (*) and find him/her proficient in those procedures and operations."

For a flight instructor certificate **without** an expiration date:
[date] /s/ J. J. Jones 987654321CFI REED 12-31-2026

For a flight instructor certificate **with** an expiration date:
[date] /s/ J. J. Jones 987654321CFI Exp. 01-31-2025

CFI-G NOTES:

> **Insert as appropriate:*
> - *Ground to1V procedures*
> - *Aero to1V procedures*
> - *Self-launch procedures*

Exemptions to this endorsement are found in FAR 61.31(j) (2).

The authorized instructor who provided the training must make this endorsement.

If the Glider pilot is adding a different launch method to their skill set, this endorsement must be made for the additional launch method.

ADDITIONAL TYPE-SPECIFIC TRAINING
FAR 61.31 (h)

"I have given Mr./Ms. _____, certificate # _____, the additional training in the systems and operational characteristics of a (airplane make/model) and find him/her proficient to act as PIC."

For a flight instructor certificate **without** an expiration date:
[date] /s/ J. J. Jones 987654321CFI REED 12-31-2026

For a flight instructor certificate **with** an expiration date:
[date] /s/ J. J. Jones 987654321CFI Exp. 01-31-2025

CFI NOTES:

The Administrator must determine the need for this (e.g. a Mitsubishi MU-2).

Training can be accomplished in the aircraft or in a Flight Simulator or Flight Training Device representative of that type of aircraft.

The authorized instructor who provided the training must make this endorsement.

REMOVAL OF NIGHT FLYING EXCEPTION
FAR 61.110 (b)(2)(ii) - Private Pilot
FAR 61.131 (b)(2)(ii) - Commercial Pilot

"I certify I have given Mr./Ms._____, certificate # _____, the night flight training required by FAR (*) for the removal of the 'night flying prohibited' limitation on his/her certificate."

For a flight instructor certificate **without** an expiration date:
[date] /s/ J. J. Jones 987654321CFI REED 12-31-2026

For a flight instructor certificate **with** an expiration date:
[date] /s/ J. J. Jones 987654321CFI Exp. 01-31-2025

CFI NOTES:

*61.109 for Private Pilot applicants, and
*61.129 for Commercial Pilot applicants

If a person receives flight training, and resides, in the State of Alaska, and has not been able to accomplish the night flying requirements per FAR 61.109, they may be issued a certificate with the limitation "Night flying prohibited." They then have 12 calendar months to accomplish the night flying requirements and to present this endorsement, upon completion of the night flying requirements, to an examiner to get the limitation removed from their certificate.

The authorized instructor who provided the training must make this endorsement.

REMOVAL OF LIMITATIONS ON BALLOON CERTIFICATES
FAR 61.115 (a) - Private Pilots
FAR 61.133 (b) - Commercial Pilots

"I certify I have given Mr./Ms. _____, certificate # _____, the additional training required by FAR (*) and attest they have the aeronautical experience and ability to satisfactorily operate a (balloon) (balloon with an airborne heater)."

For a flight instructor certificate **without** an expiration date:
[date] /s/ J. J. Jones 987654321CFI REED 12-31-2026

For a flight instructor certificate **with** an expiration date:
[date] /s/ J. J. Jones 987654321CFI Exp. 01-31-2025

CFI NOTES:

Private Pilot:
> **61.109 (h)(1) if removing a gas balloon limitation*
> **61.109 (h)(2) if removing a balloon with airborne heater limitation*

Commercial Pilot:
> **61129 (h)(4) if removing a gas balloon limitation*
> **61.129 (h)(4) if removing a balloon with airborne heater limitation*

If a practical test is taken in either type of balloon, the removal of the privilege limitation is accomplished by an authorized instructor entering this endorsement in the pilot's logbook.

The authorized instructor who provided the training must make this endorsement.

GROUND INSTRUCTOR RECURRENCY
FAR61.217

"I certify I have determined Mr./Ms. _____, Ground Instructor certificate # _____, has demonstrated knowledge in those subject areas prescribed under FAR 61.213 (a)(3) & (a)(4)."

For a flight instructor certificate **without** an expiration date:
[date] /s/ J. J. Jones 987654321CFI REED 12-31-2026

For a flight instructor certificate **with** an expiration date:
[date] /s/ J. J. Jones 987654321CFI Exp. 01-31-2025

CFI NOTES:

While at the time of this edition, ground instructor certificates do NOT expire, there are 'recency of use' limitations:

No ground instructor may exercise the privileges of a ground instructor unless within the preceding 12 calendar months they have met the requirements in FAR 61.217 (a), (b) or (c)

Any authorized instructor may make this endorsement.

PREREQUISITES FOR PRACTICAL TESTS
FAR 61.39 (a) 6

"I certify I have given Mr./Ms._____, certificate # _____, the flight instruction required by FAR 61.39 (a)(6) within the preceding two calendar months in preparation for the (type) Practical Test and find him/her prepared for the exam. He/she has demonstrated satisfactory knowledge of the subject areas shown to be deficient on his/her Airman Knowledge Test."

For a flight instructor certificate **without** an expiration date:
[date] /s/ J. J. Jones 987654321CFI REED 12-31-2026

For a flight instructor certificate **with** an expiration date:
[date] /s/ J. J. Jones 987654321CFI Exp. 01-31-2025

CFI NOTES:

The authorized instructor who provided the training must make this endorsement.

RETEST AFTER KNOWLEDGE or PRACTICAL TEST FAILURE
FAR 61.49 (a)(l)

"I certify I have given Mr./Ms. _____, certificate # _____, the additional training required by FAR 61.49(a)(l) in the areas found deficient during the (type) Knowledge/Practical Test taken on (Date) and have determined he/she is proficient to pass the (type) Knowledge/Practical Test."

For a flight instructor certificate **without** an expiration date:
[date] /s/ J. J. Jones 987654321CFI REED 12-31-2026

For a flight instructor certificate **with** an expiration date:
[date] /s/ J. J. Jones 987654321CFI Exp. 01-31-2025

CFI NOTES:

Prior to any re-examination for a Practical Test, a new FAA Form 8710-1 (8710-11 for Sport Pilot) application or a new IACRA electronic application must be completed and submitted by the applicant and signed by the recommending instructor.

The authorized instructor who provided the training must make this endorsement.

USE OF NIGHT VISION GOGGLES
FAR 61.31 (k)(l)(2)
FAR 61.66

"I certify I have given Mr./Ms. _____, pilot certificate #_____, the ground and flight training required by FAR 61.3l (k) in the normal, abnormal and emergency procedures of night vision goggles and found him/her proficient in their use."

For a flight instructor certificate **without** an expiration date:
[date] /s/ J. J. Jones 987654321CFI REED 12-31-2026

For a flight instructor certificate **with** an expiration date:
[date] /s/ J. J. Jones 987654321CFI Exp. 01-31-2025

CFI NOTES:

The authorized instructor who provided the training must make this endorsement.

Exceptions to this FAR can be found in FAR 61.31 (k) (3)

FAR 61.66 contains several sections regarding the training, retaining and proficiency requirements for the use of NVG's. Anyone contemplating their use should thoroughly familiarize themselves with the FAR.

NIGHT VISION GOGGLES PROFICIENCY CHECK
FAR 61.31 (k)
FAR 61.57 (g)
FAR61.66

"I certify I have given Mr./Ms._____, certificate # _____, the ground and flight training required by FAR 61.31 (k) and find him/her proficient in the use of night vision goggles."

For a flight instructor certificate **without** an expiration date:
[date] /s/ J. J. Jones 987654321CFI REED 12-31-2026

For a flight instructor certificate **with** an expiration date:
[date] /s/ J. J. Jones 987654321CFI Exp. 01-31-2025

CFI NOTES:

Use of NVGs have a very short currency limit. Those pilots who have not maintained currency under FAR 61.57 (f) (1) or (2) must accomplish a NVG Proficiency Check.

The authorized instructor who administered the PC must make this endorsement.

FAR 61.66 contains several sections regarding the training, retraining and proficiency requirements for the use of NVG's. Anyone contemplating their use should thoroughly familiarize themselves with this FAR.

SECOND IN COMMAND QUALIFICATION
FAR 61.55 (d)(l)(2) & 61.55 (e)(l)(2)

"I certify I have given Mr./Ms._____, certificate # _____, the appropriate ground and flight training and he/she has demonstrated the skill and knowledge required for safe operation of [aircraft type] relevant to the duties and responsibilities of a Second in Command."

For a flight instructor certificate **without** an expiration date:
[date] /s/ J. J. Jones 987654321CFI REED 12-31-2026

For a flight instructor certificate **with** an expiration date:
[date] /s/ J. J. Jones 987654321CFI Exp. 01-31-2025

CFI NOTES:

Those persons qualified to make this endorsement are listed in FAR 61.55 (d)(1)(2).

The applicant may then appear in person at the FSDO or examiner with their training records/logbook and completed FAA Form 8710-1 or IACRA equivalent.

There is no Practical Test required for the issuance of the "SIC Privileges ONLY" pilot type rating.

The authorized instructor who provided the training must make this endorsement.

TSA U.S. CITIZENSHIP
49 CFR 1552.3 (h)

"I certify that [insert student's name] has presented me with a [type of document presented], control number [relevant control or identification number] establishing the he/she is a United States citizen [or national] in accordance with 49 CFR 1552.3 (h)."

For a flight instructor certificate **without** an expiration date:
[date] /s/ J. J. Jones 987654321CFI REED 12-31-2026

For a flight instructor certificate **with** an expiration date:
[date] /s/ J. J. Jones 987654321CFI Exp. 01-31-2025

CFI NOTES:

NOTES:

THE CFI RECORDS RULE

FAR 61.189

1. A flight instructor MUST sign the logbook (or training record) of each person to whom he/she has given ground or flight training.
2. A flight instructor MUST maintain a record in a logbook or a separate document that contains the following:
   a. The name of each person whose logbook or student pilot certificate the instructor has endorsed for solo flight privileges, and the date of the endorsement.
   b. The name of each person that instructor has endorsed for a knowledge test or a practical test, and the record shall also indicate the kind of test, the date, and the results.
3. Each flight instructor must retain the records required by this section for at least three (3) years.

SAMPLE:

Date	Name
10 Oct 1915	*Manfred von Richtofen*
Test Name/Solo	Results
First Solo	*He lived!*

THE SPORT PILOT RECORDS RULE

FAR 61.423

1. As a flight instructor with a Sport Pilot rating you must:

   A. Sign the logbook of each person to whom you have given flight training or ground training.

   B. Keep a record of the name, date, & type of endorsement for:

      (i) Each person whose logbook or Student Pilot certificate you have endorsed for solo privileges.

      (ii) Each person for whom you have provided an endorsement for a knowledge test, practical test, or proficiency check, and the record must include the kind of test or check and the results.

      (iii) Each person whose logbook you have endorsed as proficient to operate:

         (a) An additional category or class of flight-sport aircraft

         (b) In Class B, C and D airspace; at an airport located in Class B, C or D airspace; and to, from, through or at an airport having an operational control tower

         (c) A light-sport aircraft that is an airplane with a Vh less than or equal to 87 knots CAS, and

         (d) A light-sport aircraft with a Vh greater than 87 knots CAS.

      (iv) Each person whose logbook you have endorsed as proficient to provide flight training in an additional category or class of light-sport aircraft

2. Within 10 days after providing an endorsement for a person to operate or provide training in an additional category and class of light-sport aircraft you must:

   A. Complete, sign and submit to the FAA the application presented to you to obtain those privileges, and

   B. Retain a copy of the form

3. You must keep the records listed in this section for 3 years.

   You may keep these records in a logbook or separate document.

Date	Name	
Test Name/Solo		Results

Date	Name	
Test Name/Solo		Results

Date	Name	
Test Name/Solo		Results

Date	Name	
Test Name/Solo		Results

Date	Name	
Test Name/Solo		Results

Date	Name	
Test Name/Solo		Results

Date	Name	
Test Name/Solo		Results

Date	Name	
Test Name/Solo		Results

Date	Name	
Test Name/Solo		Results

Date	Name	
Test Name/Solo		Results

Date	Name	
Test Name/Solo		Results

Date	Name	
Test Name/Solo		Results

Date	Name	
Test Name/Solo		Results

Date	Name	
Test Name/Solo		Results

Date	Name	
Test Name/Solo		Results

Date	Name	
Test Name/Solo		Results

Date	Name	
Test Name/Solo		Results

Date	Name	
Test Name/Solo		Results

Date	Name	
Test Name/Solo		Results

Date	Name	
Test Name/Solo		Results

Date	Name	
Test Name/Solo		Results

Date	Name
Test Name/Solo	Results

Date	Name
Test Name/Solo	Results

Date	Name
Test Name/Solo	Results

Date	Name
Test Name/Solo	Results

Date	Name
Test Name/Solo	Results

Date	Name
Test Name/Solo	Results

Date	Name
Test Name/Solo	Results

Date	Name
Test Name/Solo		Results

Date	Name
Test Name/Solo		Results

Date	Name
Test Name/Solo		Results

Date	Name
Test Name/Solo		Results

Date	Name
Test Name/Solo		Results

Date	Name
Test Name/Solo		Results

Date	Name
Test Name/Solo		Results

Date	Name
Test Name/Solo	Results

Date	Name
Test Name/Solo	Results

Date	Name
Test Name/Solo	Results

Date	Name
Test Name/Solo	Results

Date	Name
Test Name/Solo	Results

Date	Name
Test Name/Solo	Results

Date	Name
Test Name/Solo	Results

Date	Name
Test Name/Solo	Results

Date	Name
Test Name/Solo	Results

Date	Name
Test Name/Solo	Results

Date	Name
Test Name/Solo	Results

Date	Name
Test Name/Solo	Results

Date	Name
Test Name/Solo	Results

Date	Name
Test Name/Solo	Results

Date	Name	
Test Name/Solo		Results

Date	Name	
Test Name/Solo		Results

Date	Name	
Test Name/Solo		Results

Date	Name	
Test Name/Solo		Results

Date	Name	
Test Name/Solo		Results

Date	Name	
Test Name/Solo		Results

Date	Name	
Test Name/Solo		Results

Date	Name
Test Name/Solo	Results

Date	Name
Test Name/Solo	Results

Date	Name
Test Name/Solo	Results

Date	Name
Test Name/Solo	Results

Date	Name
Test Name/Solo	Results

Date	Name
Test Name/Solo	Results

Date	Name
Test Name/Solo	Results

Date	Name	
Test Name/Solo		Results

Date	Name	
Test Name/Solo		Results

Date	Name	
Test Name/Solo		Results

Date	Name	
Test Name/Solo		Results

Date	Name	
Test Name/Solo		Results

Date	Name	
Test Name/Solo		Results

Date	Name	
Test Name/Solo		Results

Date	Name	
Test Name/Solo		Results

Date	Name	
Test Name/Solo		Results

Date	Name	
Test Name/Solo		Results

Date	Name	
Test Name/Solo		Results

Date	Name	
Test Name/Solo		Results

Date	Name	
Test Name/Solo		Results

Date	Name	
Test Name/Solo		Results

Date	Name	
Test Name/Solo		Results

Date	Name	
Test Name/Solo		Results

Date	Name	
Test Name/Solo		Results

Date	Name	
Test Name/Solo		Results

Date	Name	
Test Name/Solo		Results

Date	Name	
Test Name/Solo		Results

Date	Name	
Test Name/Solo		Results

FLIGHT REVIEW & INSTRUMENT PROFICIENCY CHECKS

AFTER completing a BFR or IPC, record the fact in these pages.

Circle that which is due next, the BFR or IPC.

Once each month refer to these pages to remind you when to call your clients to set up their next appointment.

SAMPLE:

Date	Client
11 Sept 1928	*James P. Doolittle*
Phone #	BFR / IPC Due
111-222-3333	*March 1928*

Date	Client
Phone #	BFR / IPC Due

Date	Client
Phone #	BFR / IPC Due

Date	Client
Phone #	BFR / IPC Due

Date	Client
Phone #	BFR / IPC Due

Date	Client
Phone #	BFR / IPC Due

Date	Client
Phone #	BFR / IPC Due

Date	Client
Phone #	BFR / IPC Due

FLIGHT REVIEW & INSTRUMENT PROFICIENCY CHECKS

Date	Client
Phone #	BFR / IPC Due

Date	Client
Phone #	BFR / IPC Due

Date	Client
Phone #	BFR / IPC Due

Date	Client
Phone #	BFR / IPC Due

Date	Client
Phone #	BFR / IPC Due

Date	Client
Phone #	BFR / IPC Due

Date	Client
Phone #	BFR / IPC Due

Date	Client
Phone #	BFR / IPC Due

Date	Client
Phone #	BFR / IPC Due

Date	Client
Phone #	BFR / IPC Due

Date	Client
Phone #	BFR / IPC Due

Date	Client
Phone #	BFR / IPC Due

Date	Client
Phone #	BFR / IPC Due

Date	Client
Phone #	BFR / IPC Due

FLIGHT REVIEW & INSTRUMENT PROFICIENCY CHECKS

Date	Client
Phone #	BFR / IPC Due

Date	Client
Phone #	BFR / IPC Due

Date	Client
Phone #	BFR / IPC Due

Date	Client
Phone #	BFR / IPC Due

Date	Client
Phone #	BFR / IPC Due

Date	Client
Phone #	BFR / IPC Due

Date	Client
Phone #	BFR / IPC Due

FLIGHT REVIEW & INSTRUMENT PROFICIENCY CHECKS

Date	Client
Phone #	BFR / IPC Due

Date	Client
Phone #	BFR / IPC Due

Date	Client
Phone #	BFR / IPC Due

Date	Client
Phone #	BFR / IPC Due

Date	Client
Phone #	BFR / IPC Due

Date	Client
Phone #	BFR / IPC Due

Date	Client
Phone #	BFR / IPC Due

Date	Client
Phone #	BFR / IPC Due

Date	Client
Phone #	BFR / IPC Due

Date	Client
Phone #	BFR / IPC Due

Date	Client
Phone #	BFR / IPC Due

Date	Client
Phone #	BFR / IPC Due

Date	Client
Phone #	BFR / IPC Due

Date	Client
Phone #	BFR / IPC Due

Date	Client
Phone #	BFR / IPC Due

Date	Client
Phone #	BFR / IPC Due

Date	Client
Phone #	BFR / IPC Due

Date	Client
Phone #	BFR / IPC Due

Date	Client
Phone #	BFR / IPC Due

Date	Client
Phone #	BFR / IPC Due

Date	Client
Phone #	BFR / IPC Due

FLIGHT REVIEW & INSTRUMENT PROFICIENCY CHECKS

Date	Client
Phone #	BFR / IPC Due

Date	Client
Phone #	BFR / IPC Due

Date	Client
Phone #	BFR / IPC Due

Date	Client
Phone #	BFR / IPC Due

Date	Client
Phone #	BFR / IPC Due

Date	Client
Phone #	BFR / IPC Due

Date	Client
Phone #	BFR / IPC Due

FLIGHT REVIEW & INSTRUMENT PROFICIENCY CHECKS

Date	Client
Phone #	BFR / IPC Due

Date	Client
Phone #	BFR / IPC Due

Date	Client
Phone #	BFR / IPC Due

Date	Client
Phone #	BFR / IPC Due

Date	Client
Phone #	BFR / IPC Due

Date	Client
Phone #	BFR / IPC Due

Date	Client
Phone #	BFR / IPC Due

Date	Client
Phone #	BFR / IPC Due

Date	Client
Phone #	BFR / IPC Due

Date	Client
Phone #	BFR / IPC Due

Date	Client
Phone #	BFR / IPC Due

Date	Client
Phone #	BFR / IPC Due

Date	Client
Phone #	BFR / IPC Due

Date	Client
Phone #	BFR / IPC Due

Date	Client
Phone #	BFR / IPC Due

Date	Client
Phone #	BFR / IPC Due

Date	Client
Phone #	BFR / IPC Due

Date	Client
Phone #	BFR / IPC Due

Date	Client
Phone #	BFR / IPC Due

Date	Client
Phone #	BFR / IPC Due

Date	Client
Phone #	BFR / IPC Due

Date	Client
Phone #	BFR / IPC Due

Date	Client
Phone #	BFR / IPC Due

Date	Client
Phone #	BFR / IPC Due

Date	Client
Phone #	BFR / IPC Due

Date	Client
Phone #	BFR / IPC Due

Date	Client
Phone #	BFR / IPC Due

Date	Client
Phone #	BFR / IPC Due

Date	Client
Phone #	BFR / IPC Due

Date	Client
Phone #	BFR / IPC Due

Date	Client
Phone #	BFR / IPC Due

Date	Client
Phone #	BFR / IPC Due

Date	Client
Phone #	BFR / IPC Due

Date	Client
Phone #	BFR / IPC Due

Date	Client
Phone #	BFR / IPC Due

TSR 1552: TRANSPORTATION SECURITY REGULATIONS

"I certify I have completed the initial Security Awareness Training required by 49 CFR 1552 on the date specified below. I also certify I have completed the annual recurrency training on the dates specified below and this training meets the criteria in 49 CFR 1552.23 (d)."

SAMPLE:

Initial Date	Location
3 June 2024	Denver, CO
Instructor's Name	Instructor's Signature
Dennis Koontz	*Dennis Koontz*

TRANSPORTATION SECURITY TRAINING

Initial Date	Location
Instructor's Name	Instructor's Signature

Recurrent Training Date	Method
CFI Signature	CFI Certificate Number

Recurrent Training Date	Method
CFI Signature	CFI Certificate Number

Recurrent Training Date	Method
CFI Signature	CFI Certificate Number

Recurrent Training Date	Method
CFI Signature	CFI Certificate Number

Recurrent Training Date	Method
CFI Signature	CFI Certificate Number

Recurrent Training Date	Method
CFI Signature	CFI Certificate Number

TRANSPORTATION SECURITY TRAINING

Recurrent Training Date	Method
CFI Signature	CFI Certificate Number

Recurrent Training Date	Method
CFI Signature	CFI Certificate Number

Recurrent Training Date	Method
CFI Signature	CFI Certificate Number

Recurrent Training Date	Method
CFI Signature	CFI Certificate Number

Recurrent Training Date	Method
CFI Signature	CFI Certificate Number

Recurrent Training Date	Method
CFI Signature	CFI Certificate Number

Recurrent Training Date	Method
CFI Signature	CFI Certificate Number

TRANSPORTATION SECURITY TRAINING

Recurrent Training Date	Method
CFI Signature	CFI Certificate Number

Recurrent Training Date	Method
CFI Signature	CFI Certificate Number

Recurrent Training Date	Method
CFI Signature	CFI Certificate Number

Recurrent Training Date	Method
CFI Signature	CFI Certificate Number

Recurrent Training Date	Method
CFI Signature	CFI Certificate Number

Recurrent Training Date	Method
CFI Signature	CFI Certificate Number

Recurrent Training Date	Method
CFI Signature	CFI Certificate Number

TSA CITIZENSHIP
ENDORSEMENT & RECORD

"I certify I have given Mr./Ms._____, has presented to me a (type of document, i.e. U.S. birth certificate or U.S. passport) establishing that he/she is a U.S. citizen (or national) in accordance with 49 CFR 1552.3 (h)."

For a flight instructor certificate **without** an expiration date:
[date] /s/ J. J. Jones 987654321CFI REED 12-31-2026

For a flight instructor certificate **with** an expiration date:
[date] /s/ J. J. Jones 987654321CFI Exp. 01-31-2025

Date	Name
14 Oct 2008	Peggy A. Long
Document Type	
Birth Certificate	

TSA CITIZENSHIP ENDORSEMENT & RECORD

Date	Name
Document Type	

Date	Name
Document Type	

Date	Name
Document Type	

Date	Name
Document Type	

Date	Name
Document Type	

Date	Name
Document Type	

Date	Name
Document Type	

TSA CITIZENSHIP ENDORSEMENT & RECORD

Date	Name
Document Type	

Date	Name
Document Type	

Date	Name
Document Type	

Date	Name
Document Type	

Date	Name
Document Type	

Date	Name
Document Type	

Date	Name
Document Type	

TSA CITIZENSHIP ENDORSEMENT & RECORD

Date	Name
Document Type	

Date	Name
Document Type	

Date	Name
Document Type	

Date	Name
Document Type	

Date	Name
Document Type	

Date	Name
Document Type	

Date	Name
Document Type	

TSA CITIZENSHIP ENDORSEMENT & RECORD

Date	Name
Document Type	

Date	Name
Document Type	

Date	Name
Document Type	

Date	Name
Document Type	

Date	Name
Document Type	

Date	Name
Document Type	

Date	Name
Document Type	

TSA CITIZENSHIP ENDORSEMENT & RECORD

Date	Name
Document Type	

Date	Name
Document Type	

Date	Name
Document Type	

Date	Name
Document Type	

Date	Name
Document Type	

Date	Name
Document Type	

Date	Name
Document Type	

TSA CITIZENSHIP ENDORSEMENT & RECORD

Date	Name
Document Type	

Date	Name
Document Type	

Date	Name
Document Type	

Date	Name
Document Type	

Date	Name
Document Type	

Date	Name
Document Type	

Date	Name
Document Type	

TSA CITIZENSHIP ENDORSEMENT & RECORD

Date	Name
Document Type	

Date	Name
Document Type	

Date	Name
Document Type	

Date	Name
Document Type	

Date	Name
Document Type	

Date	Name
Document Type	

Date	Name
Document Type	

TSA CITIZENSHIP ENDORSEMENT & RECORD

Date	Name
Document Type	

Date	Name
Document Type	

Date	Name
Document Type	

Date	Name
Document Type	

Date	Name
Document Type	

Date	Name
Document Type	

Date	Name
Document Type	

TSA CITIZENSHIP ENDORSEMENT & RECORD

Date	Name
Document Type	

Date	Name
Document Type	

Date	Name
Document Type	

Date	Name
Document Type	

Date	Name
Document Type	

Date	Name
Document Type	

Date	Name
Document Type	

ORDER FORM

To obtain additional copies of the:

*FLIGHT INSTRUCTOR'S GUIDE TO ENDORSEMENTS, IACRA &
THE TSA*

1. Order securely online at the following websites:

   www.ColoradoSkymaster.com.

   www.amazon.com

OR

2. Send a copy of this form along with a check or money order for

$25.00 per book (postage paid) to:

Drew Chitiea
PO Box 246
Watkins, CO 80137-0246

Please inquire about dealer pricing & discounts.

Name Company_____

Address_____

City/State/ Zip_____

Email_____

Phone/Cell_____

Your comments on the back of this form are welcome!

COMMENTS

_____

_____

_____

_____

_____

_____

_____

_____

_____

_____

_____

_____

When once you have tasted flight,
You will always walk the earth with your eyes turned
skyward:
For there you have been
And there you will always be.
~ Leonardo da Vinci 1452-1519

First Man-Flight, December 17, 1903
Kitty Hawk, N. C.

Mankind's first powered takeoff, signed by the pilot (author's collection).

Aviation in itself is not inherently dangerous.
But it is terribly unforgiving of Carelessness,
Incapacity and Neglect.
~ Aviation proverb

www.ingramcontent.com/pod-product-compliance
Lightning Source LLC
Chambersburg PA
CBHW070043100426

42740CB00013B/2774